Living the Illumined Life

Living the Illumined Life

Joel S. Goldsmith

Edited by
Lorraine Sinkler

Acropolis Books, Publisher
Atlanta, Georgia

For information contact:
ACROPOLIS BOOKS, INC.
Atlanta, Georgia

www.acropolisbooks.com

Library of Congress Cataloging-in-Publication Data

Goldsmith, Joel S., 1892-1964.
  Living the illumined life / Joel S. Goldsmith ; edited By Lorraine
Sinkler.
     p. cm.
Includes bibliographical references.
  ISBN 1-889051-61-6
  1. Spiritual life. I. Sinkler, Lorraine. II. Title.
  BP610 .G641587 2002
  299'.93--dc21
                                                    2002010729

Except the Lord build the house,
they labour in vain that build it. . .

– Psalm 127

"Illumination dissolves all material ties and binds men together with the golden chains of spiritual understanding; it acknowledges only the leadership of the Christ; it has no ritual or rule but the divine, impersonal universal Love; no other worship than the inner Flame that is ever lit at the shrine of Spirit. This union is the free state of spiritual brotherhood. The only restraint is the discipline of Soul; therefore, we know liberty without license; we are a united universe without physical limits, a divine service to God without ceremony or creed. The illumined walk without fear – by Grace."

–*The Infinite Way* by Joel S. Goldsmith

Dedication

Twentieth century mystic Joel S. Goldsmith revealed to the Western world the nature and substance of mystical living that demonstrated how mankind can live in the consciousness of God. The clarity and insight of his teachings, called the Infinite Way, were captured in more than thirty-five books and in over twelve hundred hours of tape recordings that, today, perpetuate his message.

Joel faithfully arranged to have prepared from his class tapes, monthly letters which were made available as one of the most important tools to assist students in their study and application of the Infinite Way teachings. He felt each of these letters came from an ever-new insight that would produce a deeper level of understanding and awareness of truth as students worked diligently with this fresh and timely material.

Each yearly compilation of the *Letters* focused on a central theme, and it became apparent that working with an entire year's material built an ascending level of consciousness. The *Letters* were subsequently published as books, each containing all the year's letters. The publications became immensely popular as they proved to be of great assistance in the individual student's development of spiritual awareness.

Starting in 1954, the monthly letters were made availiable to students wishing to subscribe to them. Each year of the *Letters* was published individually during 1954 through 1959 and made available in book form. From 1960 through 1970 the *Letters* were published and renamed as books with the titles:

1960 Letters	*Our Spiritual Resources*
1961 Letters	*The Contemplative Life*
1962 Letters	*Man Was Not Born to Cry*
1963 Letters	*Living Now*
1964 Letters	*Realization of Oneness*
1965 Letters	*Beyond Words and Thoughts*
1966 Letters	*The Mystical I*
1967 Letters	*Living Between Two Worlds*
1968 Letters	*The Altitude of Prayer*
1969 Letters	*Consciousness Is What I Am*
1970 Letters	*Awakening Mystical Consciousness*

Joel worked closely with his editor, Lorraine Sinkler, to ensure each letter carried the continuity, integrity, and pure consciousness of the message. After Joel's transition in 1964, Emma A. Goldsmith (Joel's wife) requested that Lorraine continue working with the monthly letters, drawing as in the past from the inexhaustible tape recordings of his class work with students. The invaluable work by Lorraine and Emma has ensured that this message will be preserved and available in written form for future generations. Acropolis Books is honored and privileged to offer in book form the next eleven years of Joel's teaching.

The 1971 through 1981 *Letters* also carry a central theme for each year, and have been renamed with the following titles:

1971 Letters	*Living by the Word*
1972 Letters	*Living the Illumined Life*
1973 Letters	*Seek Ye First*
1974 Letters	*Spiritual Discernment: the Healing Consciousness*
1975 Letters	*A Message for the Ages*
1976 Letters	*I Stand on Holy Ground*
1977 Letters	*The Art of Spiritual Living*
1978 Letters	*God Formed Us for His Glory*
1979 Letters	*The Journey Back to the Father's House*
1980 Letters	*Showing Forth the Presence of God*
1981 Letters	*The Only Freedom*

Acropolis Books dedicates this series of eleven books to Lorraine Sinkler and Emma A. Goldsmith for their ongoing commitment to ensure that these teachings will never be lost to the world.

Table of Contents

1 The Now Activity of the Christ

19 First Steps On the Path of Discipleship

35 The Sword of the Spirit

53 Life Unfolding As the Fruitage of Attained Consciousness

71 Putting Off the Old Man and Rebirth

89 Building the Transcendental Consciousness

107 Preparation for Spiritual Baptism

125 The Fourth Dimension

143 From Humanhood to Divinity

161 "Call No Man Your Father Upon the Earth"

179 Teacher and Student On the Path

197 Spiritual Illumination

215 About the Series

217 Scriptural References and Notes

221 Tape Recording References

Living the Illumined Life

Chapter One

The Now Activity of the Christ

The spiritual path is the way through which we enter the spiritual life, and ultimately it leads us to that place where we know beyond all doubt that the spirit of God dwells in us and is living our life. The activity of the Spirit is always fruitful, productive of harmony, peace, joy, and abundance. In spiritual living there is no chance, nor are there accidental events of any nature.

Most persons think of going to church, to a lecture on spiritual subjects, or reading a book of spiritual wisdom as if it were a human act, even an act of their own will. This really is not the case at all because human instinct does not lead a person naturally in that direction. It is only when the activity of something greater than one's self has touched an individual's consciousness that he is led to a truth-teaching. So it is that same something that has brought you to the reading of this letter. You would not be doing this if it were not for the activity of the Spirit, the Christ, functioning in you, and functioning as your consciousness. That this Christ function as your life is the goal of spiritual living. This is the ultimate attainment.

Letting Go of This World for the Kingdom

Truth is not an easy path to walk. Many persons still have the mistaken idea that in coming to truth they are going to find their human problems quickly met and then perhaps they will dangle on some kind of a ninth cloud. The harp has been eliminated, and I am not quite sure what has taken its place. It is true that entering the spiritual path does eliminate many problems—the major discords and inharmonies of our lives—and usually very quickly. However, since eliminating problems is not the primary goal of truth, these outer harmonies indicate that we have merely entered the spiritual path at this stage. The next step to which we must look forward is the overcoming of our human pleasures, human profits, and human harmonies.

The basis for this is the Master's revelation that "My kingdom is not of this world."[1] What is the spiritual kingdom? What is the Christ-kingdom? What kind of life will we find there? On this point the Master said: "My peace I give unto you: not as the world giveth, give I unto you."[2] But this spiritual peace is not the peace of merely improved health, a doubled income, or a better home. There is something else, something more than that.

The spiritual path of life is a life into which something greater than one's self has entered. It is a life which the Christ is living, into which the Christ has entered the soul of an individual through his conscious awareness of It as his very life. And since a spiritual life is one into which the Christ has entered, the question naturally arises: How may we receive this Christ? How may we fit ourselves for the entrance of that Something into our consciousness which is to make our world new?

The Christ does make our world new. It operates in the beginning to improve our human status: It gives us better health, a better sense of supply, a greater love—a greater love for God and a much greater love for our neighbor. More than this, when the Christ enters our consciousness, It reveals that our greatest function in prayer is to pray for our enemies, to learn how to forgive seventy times seven, and how not to resist evil. The Christ creates a new world for us, first in the overcoming of our discords, but secondly in the overcoming of even the things that we call good.

It is not that there is any evil in our usual pleasures such as the theater, dancing, or sports, but with the entrance of the Christ into consciousness, we are elevated above a complete absorption in these outer amusements so that we are able to enjoy the fruits of the Spirit. There must be a mode of life in "My kingdom" so worthy of attainment that we are enabled to give up not only the pains of sense but a dependence on many of the pleasures of sense as well.

Only One Goal on the Path

In fitting ourselves for the entrance of the Christ into our consciousness, we turn to the Master for guidance and instruction. First of all, in opening our consciousness to the entrance of the Christ, we must be very sure that we do not have something in mind that we hope to gain by virtue of our attaining the realization of the Christ. We must be sure that we want the Christ, but only for the sake of the Christ—not for some purpose, not for some benefit, because that is the surest way to set up a barrier to Its entrance. We must have no goal beyond the attainment of the Christ. This is the meaning of the Master's admonition: "Therefore I say unto you, Take no thought for your life, what ye shall eat; neither for the body, what ye shall put on. . . . Seek ye the kingdom of God; and all these things shall be added unto you."[3]

We take no thought for the added things or the things that we want added, but drop all such thoughts and desire the Christ only for the sake of the Christ, that It may make our life new.

In what way? Who knows? Sometimes it takes a businessman right out of his business and a housewife right out of her home and sets them out upon a spiritual ministry. Sometimes it brings forth art, literature, or music from an individual who had no knowledge at all that these were buried within him.

Not Adding To, but Releasing from Within

The spiritual path reveals something that those living a materialistic life have never discovered and never will. In the material way of living, a person is always seeking to add something to himself, always seeking happiness, seeking prosperity, seeking success, seeking love, seeking companionship—always seeking something. It is seeking a happiness that is not to be found by seeking, because the very seeking of it makes it elude us. In the moment, however, that we stop the search for happiness, it finds us.

The spiritual life reveals that the kingdom of God is within us; whereas the material life says that we must go out and get, achieve, attain, do. The spiritual life teaches that all truth, life, love, harmony, peace, and divine grace are within, and we must open out a way for these to escape. Every great poet has found that poetry was locked up within him, but usually some particular experience has triggered an awareness that enables him to open his consciousness so that the poetry that was stored up in him—the beauty, the harmony, the grace, the love, the joy, and the peace—could flow out in forms of beauty.

So it has been the experience of those of us on the spiritual path that we must begin by understanding that the kingdom of God is within us. We are not going to gain our desire by chasing after it in the outer world or searching or seeking for it. We are not even going to find God by searching for Him: we are going to find God by resting in the assurance that the kingdom of God is already within us, and all we have to do is to open out a way for "the imprisoned splendor to escape."[4]

There is no greater splendor and no greater light than the Christ. Therefore, we accept the truth that the Christ is within us now, and it becomes our function to open our consciousness that the Christ may escape, may flow out from us in the form of harmony, healing, love, joy, beauty, the spiritual life or spiritual ministry itself. It may flow out in some form of art or music; It may come forth in some great invention or discovery. But one thing is certain, and that is that in opening our consciousness, it must be only for the realization of the Christ, with no thought in mind as to what form of harmony the Christ will reveal in us.

The Christ is the light of the world, and the Christ will reveal the divine faculties, grace, and abilities which are already established within us from the beginning and will bring these into form and expression. But to attain this, let us forget this world. Let us forget the peace that could come to us with better health, more money, or a better home. Let us forget anything and everything that pertains to this world, and let us center our attention on My kingdom, on the peace that can come from My kingdom, the joy and the beauty.

When we speak of health, harmony, or abundance, let us not translate these into terms of physical health or financial abundance. Let us keep our vision pointed toward the abundance of the Christ, the divine harmonies of the Christ, the spiritual grace, the spiritual faculties and qualities. It is true that in turn they will manifest outwardly in human good, only we must be in the position of not seeking these, but seeking only the realization of this Christ, the spirit of God, that is within us.

Only Now

In the spiritual life, there is only one time: now. There is no past and there is no future. The past can never live again under any circumstance, except as an activity of memory, and if we refuse to bring it up in our memory, it is dead: the past glories as well as the past failures, the past sins as well as the past purity. In this now of which we speak, it would be as wrong to glory in our past virtues as it would be to regret our past sins. Both the glories and the sins are gone, and we are done with them. There can be no return to them, except as an activity of memory, and in the spiritual life even the memory of them is soon lost.

The future will never come, because the only future that can ever come to us is an extension of now. It is what is transpiring in our consciousness now that will appear to us in the future that we call tomorrow. In other words, we are creating tomorrow now. There is no tomorrow that is going to come to us from outside somewhere; there is no tomorrow that can sneak up on us. The tomorrow that we experience is an extension of now, of this moment.

Sacrifice the Past

If we open our consciousness in this moment to the realization of the Christ, tomorrow will be a continuing activity of the Christ. If we persist in dwelling in memory on our virtues or our vices, tomorrow we will be met only with our past virtues and vices, and we cannot live on them, nor can we buy food or clothing with them.

It might deflate our ego a little to remember one of the well-known sayings of the metaphysical world: A practitioner is only as good as his last healing. So we can see how ridiculous it is to continue giving testimonies about the healings we were instrumental in performing last year or experienced ten years ago, when no one is interested in anything except the healings of this moment. While there are some gossips who would enjoy hashing over some of our former sins, the world in general has no interest in our past, but a very great interest in what we are now.

In the spiritual life, therefore, we do not dwell on the past. If there have been sins of omission or commission in the past, we repent of them in some moment of now; we regret that they ever had to be or that we were ever an instrument for their expression, and then dismiss them. "Neither do I condemn thee: go, and sin no more."[5] What Jesus was saying was, "Let the past drop." But he could have gone on and said, "Forget also your good deeds of the past, because they cannot be relived." As a matter of fact, the good we do lives on forever in effect, therefore we need not dwell on it. "Now are we the sons of God."[6] We need dwell only on now, and to abide in this truth makes it a continuing experience into all of the future.

The Future, an Extension of Consciousness Now

The Master revealed clearly in his lessons on spiritual healing and living that we are to abide in the Word and let the Word abide in us. This is the pattern of spiritual living: to abide in the Word *now*. In this nowness, however, we cannot put off thinking about truth until tonight when we are ready to retire because this is the moment, the moment in which the call for healing enters our consciousness. It is now and here.

We especially should be interested only in this second of time because it is this second of time that is going to determine our tomorrow. Tomorrow is an extension of our consciousness of this moment, and a divine grace or truth received in our consciousness now will externalize itself in some moment of what we might call the future, but which really is not the future: it is but an extension of now.

"Ye are the temple of God,"[7] ye are the temple of God now. "The place whereon thou standest is holy ground"[8] now. Here where we are now, God is, and the voice of God whispers: "Son, thou art ever with me, and all that I have is thine."[9] As we accept this truth in our consciousness now, it becomes a continuing manifestation and expression. As we abide in the truth that "I and my Father are one.[10] . . . He that seeth me seeth him that sent me,"[11] this will become a continuing experience, because it is what we are entertaining in consciousness now that constitutes our tomorrow and tomorrow's tomorrow. Always in the now, we are building what the world calls the future, but which we understand to be but an extension of now.

The Power of the Son of God

Let me give you the word *power* to contemplate. Do you realize that it was the Christ-power that healed the sick? It was not a man: it was the Christ-power. It was not a man who forgave the sinner: it was the Christ-power that forgave the sinner; it was the Christ-power that multiplied the loaves and fishes; it was the Christ-power that walked over the waves of human error, mortal discords; it was the Christ-power that brought about Resurrection and Ascension.

This Christ is embodied in you; this Christ is the Son of God in you, the spirit of God that dwells in you. It begins to come into manifestation upon your recognition and your acknowledgment of It. "In all thy ways acknowledge him."[12] Acknowledge the presence of the Christ within you, and then a miracle takes place.

In the material sense of life, power is outside of you: the power of climate and weather, the power of infection, the power of boom or panic times, the power of peace or war time, the power of sin, the power of disease. All these powers are out here, acting upon you. But all this ceases in the moment that you acknowledge that Christ dwells in you because now all power is given unto you. God gave man dominion over everything on the earth, above the earth, and beneath the earth. God gave man dominion through the son of God which is in you.

Why then has the world been bereft of this power? The

Hebrews were separated from it because they never acknowledged that the Messiah, the Christ, had come. The Christians also have been without the Christ because they acknowledged that the Christ came for thirty-three years and then left them, and they are now waiting for the second coming. Therefore, both the Hebrews and the Christians are without the Christ—one waiting for the Christ and the other waiting for the return of the Christ, but both acknowledging an absence of the Christ.

The mistake of the early Hebrews was that they expected their Messiah to be a general and a king who would go out with an army to set them free. So when the Messiah came, they did not recognize Him, nor did they see that His kingdom was not of this world.

Here and now, acknowledge that the Christ dwells in you. God did not send you to earth without that indwelling Christ, for that would be equivalent to turning you loose on earth into a world of howling lions. It is we who have abandoned the Christ within us: the Christ has not abandoned us. We have abandoned the God of our fathers: God has not abandoned us.

Since nothing can happen to you except through your own consciousness, you cannot benefit by the presence of the Christ except by an acknowledgment within you that Christ dwells in you. Whatever is to take place in your life must take place through the activity of your consciousness. The Master said, "Ye shall know the truth, and the truth shall make you free."[13] You must know the truth that Christ dwells in you, and that the function of the Christ in you is to heal the sick, raise the dead, feed the hungry, forgive the sinner.

Acknowledge that through this indwelling Christ you can do all things. There is no power outside of you to act upon you. Do not misunderstand that statement. There is much power in the world to act on human beings, on those who have not acknowledged that Christ dwells in them. But in the moment you accept the indwelling Christ, the Christ lives your life. It is a Presence that goes before you to "make the crooked places straight,"[14] and then you are not living your own life exclusively: you have an invisible Partner, a senior Partner, a Partner of power. It is not a power that goes out to destroy your enemies, not a power that goes out with the sword, not a power that acts as a general or a king. The power of the Christ that is within you is the "still small voice."[15] God is not in the whirlwind; God is not in the sins of this world, or the diseases of this world; God is not out there in bombs: God is in the still small voice.

The Christ Functions Through the Still Small Voice

The activity of the Christ is made manifest on earth through the still small voice which you hear. Whether or not you hear it audibly is of no importance. The point is that at the moment of your acceptance of the Christ, your attention is turned inward in an acknowledgment that the Christ is within you, and you let It speak through Its gentle voice. When It speaks, the earth melts; the armies of the aliens destroy themselves.

The Christ does not go out to destroy armies: the Christ utters Its still small voice, and whether the enemy is a person or a condition, it destroys itself, not by might or by power, but by this still small voice. So the spiritual life entails first the acknowledgment:

> Christ dwells in me. God has planted His son within
> my consciousness, and as of old, Its function is to
> enlighten me, to teach me, to preach the gospel to
> me. Its function is to be my bread, meat, wine,
> and water, the source of my inspiration. *

---

* Spontaneous meditations came to Joel during periods of uplifted consciousness and are not in any sense to be used as affirmations, denials, or formulas. They have been inserted from time to time to serve as examples of the free flowing of the Spirit. As the reader practices the Presence, he, too, in exalted moments, will receive ever new and fresh inspiration as the outpouring of the Spirit. –Ed.

How is It to function? Through the still small voice. This it is that enables you to live the life of withinness.

> The kingdom of Allness is within me.
> I do not allow myself to be so busy out here
> in the world that I forget my conscious oneness
> with that Allness. I perform everything that is right
> for me to do, but without concern,
> because I know now that the fruitage comes because
> of this inner Grace, this inner stillness and peace.

Now in this moment, so that it may be a continuing experience, realize that your life is to be lived by Grace, not by might or by power. You will still perform every function in your home, business, or profession, but you will perform it with the understanding that there is a *He* within you that performs everything that is given you to do. Always you will live from the within to the without, always you will live in a continued remembrance:

> Christ dwells in me. I let It perform
> Its work; I let It go before me.

Do not try to empower It; do not try to make It work! The Christ can use you, but you cannot use the Christ. Can you hear It in those moments when you relax, when you rest in the assurance?

> *I* will never leave you or forsake you; *I* will be with
> you unto the end of the world. *I* am your bread, and
> meat, and wine, and water. *I* am the resurrection.

Do you not realize that this *I* you read about in scripture is the Christ which was revealed to human consciousness two thousand years ago and has never left the earth? It has always been available to every individual who could open his consciousness to It. Do not believe that the Messiah has not come, or that you must wait for the second coming. It is here and now.

Recognizing the Christ-Activity in Periods of Barrenness

God does not work in the past or in the future: God works only in the now. Think now of what beauty and fruition are being prepared in the bushes and trees in your gardens! Think of what is being prepared now that will appear in May and June! The activity of God in the now, functioning in the now and continuing in the now, brings forth in May and June the flowers and the fruits. The activity of God must be working in the now. The activity of God is not going to bring us any fruits yesterday. God does not function in the past; the Christ does not function in the past or in the future: It is functioning now, and whatever appears in your garden or on your trees in the future is because of the activity of the Christ now.

Your recognition of the activity of the Christ in you now is what will appear as the fruitage in your life next week, next month, next season, next year. At some particular moment of life, you must acknowledge the indwelling Christ, and then continue to abide in that word, the Christ. If your particular life is barren at this moment—physically, mentally, morally, or financially—it makes no difference. If there are any barren spots in your life, your recognition of the activity of the Christ now will in this moment set your new crop in motion. Then it is only a matter of abiding in the Word and letting the Word abide in you until the fruitage appears.

Let the Seed Take Root

Every word of truth is a seed of truth. It is not truth itself. The Master told us of the three states of consciousness: the barren soil in which the seeds of truth will not bear fruit; the rocky soil which may accept this seed and develop it a little but as soon as temptation comes—a strong wind or a tough problem—it gives up. And then there is the fertile soil. Seeds of truth which are sown in that soil, taken into your consciousness and lived with, become the proof of whether or not your soil is fertile.

If you do not hear this message at all or if it meets with no response in you, your consciousness may be barren insofar as truth is concerned. If, however, you hear this word and receive it in your consciousness and you find that later on some part of this message returns to your consciousness, if you ponder occasionally the truths that you read, if you have your periods of meditation and remember, again and again, the truths that have entered your consciousness, then you are fertile soil, and you may expect rich fruitage.

Abide in the Word; let the Word abide in you; and you are on the spiritual path. Then you will discover that there is no such thing as a past, but that every moment of your present is a continuing experience into what the calendar calls the future. There is no such thing as one day ending and another day beginning. Those are just divisions that are made on calendars, and those of you who have been up until midnight some nights can bear witness to the fact that there is no division at midnight: it is just the same rhythm taking place all the time, and it is always now. It is always now in this Kingdom. Therefore, that which you have accepted now is the continuing experience of the Christ, and the fruitage appears in its season.

Spiritual living really means living in the word of God. On the spiritual path, you are living by every word of truth that has been planted in your consciousness, so that you dwell in it and permit it to dwell in you and bear fruit. The spiritual life is not seeking a power to do anything for you in this life. The spiritual life has nothing to do with the using of a power; the spiritual life is an acknowledgment of a life by Grace, not by might and not by power, but by the still, small voice, not using It; letting It use you.

ACROSS THE DESK

As the calendar announces the opening of a New Year, we have a good opportunity to meditate on the nowness of being which we know is present every minute of each day, a principle so clearly brought out in this letter. The world celebrates a New Year in the hope that it will bring peace and tranquility to a world filled with strife, dissension, and discord. We know that this hope will be fulfilled only when the light of Truth has permeated the consciousness of a sufficient number of dedicated souls, so that they can lift the world out of its hypnotic spell, and when enough love has been poured forth to dispel the darkness, the dream that holds the world in its grip.

Let us be diligent in our work for the world, for only when the spiritually minded unite with their Source and are thus able to see this earth here and now as heaven will this harmony be realized. Since now is the only time, this harmony is already here, and we need only recognize its presence. Then we will always have a happy New Year.

TAPE RECORDED EXCERPTS
Prepared by the Editor

At one time or other, we have all known deep fear, sometimes unaccountable fear, but nonetheless chilling fear which has held us in the most vicious kind of bondage. Does not this fear usually stem from the belief that our good is dependent upon something or some person out here in the world or that there is some condition out here that can jeopardize our very life? We have forgotten that the issues of life are in our consciousness and that within us is the power and dominion.

These excerpts from the recordings give us a hint as to the basic cause of our fears and how to go about releasing them.

Fear

"Fear is a universal thing. It is based on the belief that we have a separate life and that it can be destroyed. This universal fear, which we pick up through our antenna of the mind, is what is disturbing us, not the disease. There never was a disease that had any power even to cause us pain: our fear of the disease and what it will do to us is where the trouble lies. . . .

"There isn't any condition. . . that you can meet in life that will not respond to the understanding that underneath that whole condition is fear. We all fear to be annihilated; we fear disease only because it will lead to death. If we were not sure that disease leads to death, what would we care about disease? If it didn't have power, that would be the end of it. We fear because we fear the extinction of our life. We fear lack because we may freeze or starve.

"Fear grips the world as a universal claim. . . But mark this well: fear is not a power. The moment you realize that, you have taken the sting out of fear and made it ineffective and inoperative, and you have set an individual free in his spiritual identity. We need to lose fear of external powers.

"I wish you could see the vision that surrounds a group when fear has been handled and removed, not by declaring that God is all or that God is love, but by an inner realization that God alone is the only power, and that fear, whether individual or collective, is not power. . . . Never tell a person to stop fearing; never tell him there is nothing to fear, because he wouldn't be fearing if he could accept that; but silently within yourself smile and realize the nature of fear as nothing, the nature of fear as powerlessness. . . . Withdraw the power from the fear of the condition or the person, and you have met the situation, not only that particular situation, but you have spiritualized your consciousness to the extent that never again will you fear 'fear' quite so deeply."

Joel S. Goldsmith, "There Is No Power in Fear,"
The First Steinway Hall Closed Class.

"As long as one's thought is centered on the attainment of health, supply, safety, or security, the possibility of overcoming fear isn't very great. The reason for the fear must be eliminated before the fear itself can be overcome. If a person is fearing a condition of his heart, there is no use to tell him to stop fearing for his life. . .or for his heart because the heart has become the symbol of life to him. . . It must first be brought to light that the heart is not the source of life before the fear of the heart can be given up. . . Sometimes fear is quickly overcome in the realization that the heart does not give life, but that it is life that animates the heart. . . Life functions the heart.

"Freedom from fear is attained by overcoming the conditions that have produced fear. Once you stop fearing your heart, you begin to enter a higher sense of life because then you find the change that takes place when you realize that your life is not dependent on your heart, and you begin to live independently of your heart. You begin to live without a thought of heart entering your mind, and then find that the heart is governed harmoniously by life, and you wonder how it happened."

Joel S. Goldsmith, "Transparency for God,"
The First Maui Lectures.

"Do you see why it is necessary, first to establish yourself in the absolute conviction that there is a 'My kingdom,' a spiritual kingdom, and that 'nothing that defileth. . . or maketh a lie' can ever enter that spiritual kingdom of God and His spiritual universe and spiritual man? You must first establish the fact that 'I and my Father are one,' the conscious realization of your oneness with God, your oneness with spiritual perfection. Then from there on you are dealing only with the world of appearances. . . . You are not dealing with people or conditions: you are dealing with the world of appearances.

"The illusion here may be a lake, and the illusion there may be a city, but it is all illusion, and the substance of an illusion is nothingness, whether it appears as a lake or a building. You will eventually discover that the substance of illusion is the same whether the claim is a cold, a headache, a cancer, consumption, a broken bone, poverty, or unemployment. . . . It is nothingness, the 'arm of flesh,' appearance. Behind it is the activity of a universal malpractice or hypnotism which is produced by the universal belief in two powers."

Joel S. Goldsmith, "Infinite Way Healing Principles," *The 1962 Princess Kaiulani Open Class.*

"Whatever we put in motion has a reverse action. Whatever of good we do returns good to us; whatever of evil, wrong, or error we do returns as that to us. When we realize, however, that I can do neither good nor evil, I break the karma. . . . When I realize that I am but the transparency for God to flow through—I am but the instrument for God's good to reach mankind; I am but the instrument for the blessings of my home, my family, my friends, my practice, my student body, or the world—when I realize that I am but a point in consciousness through which God's grace is permitted to flow to bless those receptive and responsive to It, I have no responsibility for being good and I have no possibility of being too bad. The little human faults will remain with all of us, certainly, because we are still a part and parcel of that ancient Adamic belief in two powers.

"In the degree that we realize, 'I can neither do good nor evil: I am but the transparency through which God appears; I am the instrument through which God's grace is flowing,' then we have no qualities of good or evil, and then we have no good karma and we have no bad karma: we are just spiritual offspring of God, being eternally the son of God. That is being neither good nor evil: that is just being perfect. . . ."

Joel S. Goldsmith, "The Nature of Consciousness,"
The 1960 Melbourne Closed Class.

Chapter Two

First Steps On the Path
of Discipleship

Truth has been presented to the world throughout all ages, and by this time it would seem that everyone should know the truth, but there are very few who have had even the tiniest glimpse of it. I would count myself fortunate if I could say that I had attained a grain of truth, because in my heart I know how very much less than that I have attained, and I also know why.

Truth is always veiled, and it has never been presented except in a form that is veiled. The veil, however, is not necessarily for the purpose of concealing truth. In some cases, it is to make it possible for those seeking truth to understand it. To some, it might seem that the more clearly truth is stated, the more it will be understood, but that is not true.

Why and How Truth Is Veiled

If truth were presented in its stark form, I can assure you that everyone would walk away from it and say, "Well, I can swallow a lot, but not that." Truth will never be accepted by those hearing it with the human ear alone. There must be the development of an inner ear, an inner eye, and an inner perception in order to respond to truth. The work of the spiritual path is to develop that inner ear and inner eye.

Moses veiled the truth, but Christ Jesus took away that veil. Nevertheless, when Jesus rent the veil, the people of his day would not accept the truth he revealed. Instead they crucified him. All outward forms of worship, such as the ceremonies carried on in churches and cathedrals, are in reality veils. Truth is not to be found in these religious observances but lies hidden in the ceremony and the ritual, awaiting our discovery. If truth were presented unveiled, most persons would walk away from it with the comment, "That above all things cannot be truth." The ceremonies, rites, and rituals are given so that a person can look behind the scenes, dig deep, and perceive the nature of what is being presented to him, and then eventually he comes face to face with truth and realizes, "Whereas I was blind, now I see."[1]

"The world is new to every soul when Christ has entered into it."[2] This has been true of everyone throughout all time who has had the experience of the Christ. As long as we remain human beings, "the natural man,"[3] we are not "subject to the law of God, neither indeed can be,"[4] and "receiveth not the things of the spirit of God."[3] It is only when Christ has entered in that we have the capacity to receive truth, to know and to respond to truth.

When the Veils Drop Away, There Are No Contradictions in Truth

It has puzzled a great part of the world, why, since there is a God, we suffer the sins, the wars, the lacks, and injustices that continue on this human plane. Where is God in the earthquake? Where is God in all of these things? Scripture provides the answer to that, too. "The Lord was not in the wind: and after the wind an earthquake; but the Lord was not in the earthquake."[5] God is not in the falling airplane; God is not in the sinking ship. Naturally, the thought comes that all this contradicts other parts of scripture that tell us that God is everywhere equally present. These conflicts, not only in scripture but in all truth-writing, can be reconciled only when some of the veils drop away, and they will drop away in proportion as we search within ourselves.

Each one of us gains a tremendous benefit from the study of the writings of those who have attained spiritual consciousness, but these writings are merely helps. They are not the answer; they are not the Christ; they are not God: they are merely helps that enable us to dig deeper within ourselves until Truth reveals Itself.

We are told that the kingdom of God is within us. But how little time we spend within ourselves each day trying to bring forth that hidden God, that indwelling Christ! Throughout the New Testament both the Master and Paul emphasize our oneness with the Father, with that spirit of God that dwells in us. We have spent much time thinking about the Father that dwelt in Jesus, but very little time trying to bring forth the Father that dwells in us. Paul has assured us in many places that the Christ lives in us.

This spiritual spark, that which we call the Son of God, the Christ, or the Father, it has been revealed, dwells in us. But this is not an out-and-out statement of truth. It also is a veiled statement. The out-and-out statement of truth cannot be given in its unveiled form to those not prepared for it. When the Master stood before Pilate and Pilate asked, "What is truth?"[6] there is no record of the Master's answering. Had we been in Jesus' place, we might have thought, "Here is a wonderful opportunity to convert Pilate," and immediately told him all we knew about truth.

The Master knew, however, that there was no use presenting truth to the unprepared state of consciousness, because that state of consciousness could not receive it. He did not hesitate, however, to say to his disciples, "I am. . . the truth,"[7] because he was talking to those he felt had already developed enough of spiritual consciousness so that when truth was presented to them, they would be able to accept it. Later events proved that they received it only in part.

The New World of the Christ

"The world is new to every soul when Christ has entered into it." There is a period in our experience when the Christ has not entered into us, when we are only the "natural man," mortal man, not under the law of God, not able to receive the truth, in fact, ready at all times to reject it. Yet this world, which has in it so much of sorrow, so much of disaster, so much of woe, becomes new, *new* when the Christ has entered in. It becomes a world free of the world's discords and inharmonies.

The Master pointed out that as we abide in this truth and have this truth abiding in us, we bear fruit richly.[8] On the other hand, when we are not abiding in the truth and the truth is not abiding in us, we are as a branch of a tree that is cut off, withers, and dies.[8] These are the two sides of the coin of our existence. There is that side in your life and in my life before the Christ enters in, that time when we are subject to all the conditions of this world: to its sins, its diseases, its accidents, to every phase of its inharmony.

Then there is that side of our life after the Christ has entered in, when the evils of this world no longer come nigh our dwelling place.[9] Of course, there are the thousands at our left and the thousands at our right who will keep right on experiencing the discords and inharmonies of this world, and there is not much we can do about it. There are those thousands who live as branches of a tree that are cut off and wither and die, and there is not much we can do about that either. They may be husband, wife, parents, or children.

One of the tragedies of this life is that so often one or two persons in a family grasp this truth and then have to stand by and witness members of their own families and their friends continuing to suffer from the evils of this world, knowing all the time how simple it would be if they had the capacity to be of those who no longer suffer these evils, or at least whose sufferings have been reduced by eighty or ninety percent.

It has not yet been given to any of us to realize one hundred percent of the Christ-freedom, and perhaps it is best so, because this gives us the compassion and that degree of love for our fellow man who has not attained so that we do everything in an effort to help him awaken.

Do Not Be Afraid To Ask Questions

As long as we are on the spiritual path, the greatest blessing that can come to us will be not to accept anything blindly, not to act on blind faith, but to continue to question. As a truth-student, it is legitimate to question without being labeled a doubter. We can question without being afraid that we are being untrue to what has already been given us.

The first questions that come to my mind as I consider the statement, "The world is new to every soul when Christ has entered into it," are: How does Christ come to my consciousness? What can I do that the Christ may enter in? Is there anything I can do, or is it a matter of just waiting for some act of Grace, and suffering it to be so now? Can I be of any help to myself in bringing the Christ into my consciousness that I may know this indwelling Spirit? Or even granted that I have had an experience of the Christ, that I have witnessed God's grace in some of my affairs, is there anything that I can do to have a greater experience of the Christ? Is there anything I can do to have this indwelling Presence consciously with me constantly?

Can I ever arrive at the place Paul described: "I live; yet not I, but Christ liveth in me?"[10] Can I arrive at that place where I no longer have to take thought for my life, what I eat, what I drink, wherewithal I am clothed? Can I do this?

These are legitimate questions that do not indicate doubt. Rather they indicate that I am a thinker, not just a blind believer, not just a sheep ready to be hornswoggled into any path that comes along. I am a thinker, and I know what I want. I want the experience of the Christ. I want to be able to live, move, and have my being in God. I want to know that I live, yet not I, but that this Christ, this spirit of God, dwells in me. Therefore, I find it legitimate to question and to ask, "What more can I do?"

The moment that I ask this question, I am ready for the answer, and that answer will appear to me because I have asked the question, not from the standpoint of merely wanting to live an easy life, but because I really want to enter into the Christ-life. I know in advance that the way is not easy. The way is straight and narrow. From the Master, I know also that "strait is the gate, and narrow is the way, which leadeth unto life, and few there be that find it."[11] I know that it is a difficult path, and that even the disciples fell down in the Master's hour of trial, even they, after having had three years of his constant presence.

When I say, "How shall I go about this? What can I do?" I am seeking the way for something more than merely to get a healing or increase my supply. I am not thinking in terms of the Christ entering in so as to heal my headache or the Christ entering in so that I may have a little greater income. No, no! There has to be spiritual integrity behind the question. There has to be something of a desire to know God; there has to be a sincere desire to follow the spiritual path, even if it has some thorns in it. There will be roses, yes, but there will be some thorns for awhile. There will be some blessings, yes, but there will be trials for awhile.

The New World of Responsibilities

When we have attained this Christ, one of the first things we learn is that it is not given to us in order that we may sit down and revel on cloud nine for the rest of our days. It is given to us in order that we may go out on the path of discipleship and help others to attain the same light. No one is ever going to receive this grace of God or the visitation of the Christ just for the purpose of enabling him to retire to the country and live a beautiful life of ease. It does not work that way. We know that of those who have much, much is demanded. Of those who receive even a grain of truth, demands are immediately made upon them. So we know what we are doing when we ask this question: "How shall I go about experiencing the Christ?"

In the beginning, when it was evident that calls for help would be made upon that Christ, my answer was that I would not ask who it was, what it was, or how much it was, but if it were a legitimate call upon the Christ, I would respond to that call. It has been that way, and I know now, through the many students who have walked this way, that this must be the attitude: I open myself to the Christ, and I am ready for that Christ to be called upon through me. If and when I receive this Christ, I am ready to serve It. I recognize that this Christ is not going to be given to me for some special dispensation to set me apart from mankind. If I receive It, It will be for the purpose of being a light unto those still in darkness. I am not going to be able to choose that it will be only the righteous that I will serve, only the healthy, or only the wealthy.

When this Christ calls, It draws to Itself the sick and the maimed: physically, mentally, morally, financially. It calls to Itself all who are in darkness, all who are suffering from the problems of this world, and the Christ that has been realized answers all of them, never refusing to respond.

In the very moment when we turn to the Christ, we know

that It is to produce for us a new world. When It is attained, It will give us that world: a new world of obligations, a new world of duties, a new world of responsibilities, as well as a new world of safety, security, peace, joy, and abundance, but not in the ways of this world.

Relinquish All Desire for a More and Better "This World"

Seeking to have more and better of this world is where we create the first barrier to the entrance of the Christ. If I am praying for any of the good things of this world, I am praying amiss, for the Christ-peace is not the peace that this world can give. "My kingdom is not of this world."[12] Therefore, if I am praying for a multiplication of the things of this world, I am praying amiss. This gives us the first clue or first principle as to how to open ourselves to receive the Christ. If we are serious, if we are desirous of experiencing the Christ and wanting to know the harmonies and the peace of the Christ, we must put out of our thought any of the human things that we lack or have heretofore desired or wanted. There must be a turning away from all that with this attitude:

> I seek the realization of the indwelling Christ. I seek
> to know God's grace, His Son in me, that I may be
> fulfilled with the peace that passes understanding,
> that I may receive within me the Christ-kingdom,
> that I may experience the peace that the Christ gives,
> that I may know the world anew.

Into our meditation, we permit no thought of health, companionship, safety, or security to enter. These we shut out. Instead, we are seeking a spiritual kingdom, which the Master called "My kingdom." We do not know what it is like until we have experienced it, what its joys are, its fulfillment, or what its duties and responsibilities are. Nevertheless, we seek it and want it. I want to know what the Master meant when he spoke of "My kingdom" and "My peace." I want to know what he meant when he said, "Put up again thy sword."[13] We are not going to gain this peace with a sword; we are not going to gain "my kingdom" by fighting for it. We let this Christ function in us, not according to the will of man or the way of man, but according to the will of God and the way of God.

Seek Only Spiritual Wholeness

If I pray, "Father, prosper me," I am not talking about being prospered in dollars or pounds: I am talking about being prospered with His spirit, with the fullness of His spirit, with His grace. If I pray, "Make me whole," I am not talking about the pains of my flesh. When I pray, "Make me whole," it is that I may be made whole in His image and likeness.

Let me know myself as I am, the child of God.
Let me know my spiritual identity. Let me recognize
my real Self, not this caricature that I see in a mirror.
I want to see myself as I am, face to face,
in the image and likeness of God.

Thus I pray, but I am praying only for the things of the Spirit, only for the grace of God, only for the virtues and the fullness of the Christ. I am taking no thought for what I shall eat, what I shall drink, or wherewithal I shall be clothed. I am taking no thought for my physical well-being. I am turning away from the appearance, and I am asking for spiritual light:

Open my eyes that I may see. Open my ears
that I may hear. Open my consciousness that I may
receive the Christ, the fullness of the Son of God,

that I no longer live according to my idea of living,
but that I permit the Christ, the spirit of God, to
dwell in me, live in me, and live my life for me.

Spiritual Grace, the Goal

One of the great veils that has come between us and our
spiritual destiny is the fact that we are trying to hold on to the
human sense of life while at the same time praying for spiritual
Grace. We are trying to get rid of the evils of human existence,
hold on to the good things of human existence, and at the same
time pray, "Christ, live my life." Ah, no! Let us remove that barrier now, remove that veil now, and take no thought for what
tomorrow is going to bring to us. Instead, let us hold ourselves
in readiness so that if the Christ enters in and changes our plans
for tomorrow, we are ready for them to be changed. Let us not
have such a schedule ahead of us that we would have to answer
the Christ by saying, "Come back next week."

What I am trying to remove is the veil that separates us
from our spiritual attainment. Always at first the veil is the
clinging to the human good and that innate desire to get rid of
the human evil, instead of forgetting or ceasing from "man,
whose breath is in his nostrils,"[14] even if he is a good or a healthy
one, and holding steadfastly to one goal: I know now that there
is a kingdom which, as a human being, I have never glimpsed.
I know that there is a peace which has nothing whatsoever to do
with human health or human wealth, and my goal now is seeking this spiritual kingdom and this spiritual Grace.

Anxiety and Concern Act As Barriers

If I cling to this human world, I have to use the methods of
this human world: all its trickery, all its weapons, physical and
mental. But in the moment that my goal changes and I seek the

kingdom of God and His righteousness, I can put up both my physical sword and my mental sword, and be at peace.

I am not seeking to unseat the administration in Downing Street, Washington, or Pretoria. I am not seeking to unseat the Conservatives, the Socialists, the Republicans, or the Democrats: I am seeking God's government. Therefore, I am not thinking at this moment of human changes in government. When election day comes, of course I will pray, "God, guide me that I may vote in the right direction, or at least in the highest, nearest right that is possible," but that is all. For the rest of my life, I am not going to concern myself with human government, but with God's government, that we may experience God's government on earth as it is in heaven, God's government manifest through the men we elect to office. But let us not think of the men: let us think of the kingdom of God.

We who have come to the path of discipleship are engaged in seeking to know God, seeking God-realization, seeking to experience something of the kingdom of God and the grace of God. We continue to live in the ordinary human fashion, but without anxiety and concern. We cannot carry anxiety and concern into the spiritual realm, because these too, act as barriers. Let us forget mother, father, sister, and brother, not forget them in the human sense but forget them in the sense of not letting them intrude into our spiritual activities. Let us seek the kingdom of God wholeheartedly. Let us acknowledge that there is a spiritual kingdom, there is a spiritual Grace, and that the "natural man" will never know these.

As long as we are seeking only human betterment, we will never know that kingdom and that Grace. But now we put aside our childish way of just adding to our human good, and we recognize that there is a spiritual kingdom called *My* kingdom, which is not of this world. There is a peace, *My* peace, which the Spirit can give which is not of this world.

I know that there is a being which I am who can be under

the law of God, under the grace of God, but that being, that man, is not my human selfhood. My human selfhood is the natural man that is not under the law of God and who receives not the things of God. But there is the man I am, some part of me that is the child of God, knowing the kingdom of God, experiencing the peace that passes human understanding. This is my goal.

Open Consciousness to Receive God

To attain the goal, I open my consciousness specifically many times throughout the day; and certainly several times throughout the evening, I consciously open my consciousness and keep it attuned to the voice of God:

"Speak, Lord; for Thy servant heareth."[15]
I am ready to receive the kingdom of God,
the grace of God. I seek only spiritual wisdom,
spiritual love, spiritual light, spiritual truth, spiritual
abundance, spiritual harmony, spiritual security,
spiritual safety, all of which are embraced
under the grace of God, the law of God.

"Thou wilt keep him in perfect peace, whose mind is stayed on thee."[16] In thus opening ourselves in a state of receptivity to Grace, we are developing a new faculty, the ability, at all times and at any time, to open ourselves to the presence of God.

Where the spirit of the Lord is, there is fulfillment, fullness of joy, fullness of life, fullness of protection. Where is the spirit of the Lord? Certainly, it is not in the whirlwind; it is not in human thinking or in human hoping. Where is the presence of God? Where consciousness is specifically open to receive God.

God is where God is realized, and usually God is realized when we have come to the end of the human rope. That is why it is sometimes so much easier to heal the incurable. They have surrendered every single trace of hope and faith in any human means, and when they come to that place, they open their consciousness wholeheartedly to receive the grace of God.

> Father, speak! Thy grace is my sufficiency;
> Thy will be done in me; Thy kingdom come
> to my earth just as it is in heaven. I am shutting
> my eyes to human help; I am consciously
> opening my consciousness to Thy spirit.

In this way we open ourselves now, today, and for all time to come, consciously to receive God, consciously to receive His Son, consciously to receive His kingdom, consciously to receive His grace. The very first step in the spiritual life is to open consciousness specifically to a Presence and a peace that heretofore we have not known. We ourselves must open our consciousness to receive it.

Give Yourself Wholeheartedly to the Search

God is omnipresence, but God is available only where consciousness is open to receive God, and it must be done consciously, not in some offhand way like, "Oh, yes, I want God." When we seek God, we seek with our whole heart and soul and mind. When we seek God, we leave behind all else: all concerns, all worries, all human problems. When we seek God, we give ourselves to that seeking with far greater intensity than if we were seeking the North Pole, the South Pole, an oil well, or a gold mine. In seeking God, we give ourselves—the entire fiber of our being, our entire attention, our entire longing—to that one end of knowing His presence, feeling His grace until it becomes of such intensity that our whole heart, soul, and mind are stayed on God. Then the peace that passes understanding comes as the fruitage of it.

"There shall no sign be given."[17] The signs only follow the Christ-experience. Saul of Tarsus had no sign of the Christ. Only after the awakening did he have the signs following. So it has been with everyone on the spiritual path. No one is given a sign in advance to prove to him that this is the right way. No one receives any kind of assurance that he is going to have health, wealth, and happiness. Nothing happens in advance. All signs *follow* after this inner awakening has come, this inner spiritual light.

The object of our brief periods of meditation is to be alert to that Presence within, in the attitude, "Here I am. Speak, Lord!" This opening of our consciousness is the purpose of our meditation periods—opening our consciousness specifically that we may receive Him.

Attaining Our Birthright of Christhood

When we have received the Christ, we receive a new consciousness. The old man dies; a new man is born; a new experience takes place; and the world appears different to us. We give to the world in a different way, and the world gives back to us in a new way. It is a whole new world, and it is for this reason that we are constantly opening ourselves, so that even if we have received in a measure, we want to keep on receiving until we have received the fullness of the stature of manhood in Christ Jesus, until we have attained the full and complete Christhood which is our natural birthright.

"Know ye not that ye are the temple of God, and that the spirit of God dwelleth in you?[18]. . . Know ye not that your body is the temple of the Holy Ghost?[19]. . . We are the children of God,"[20] full and complete children, full and complete heirs! At first we experience this only in a tiny measure, but our birthright is full Christhood, full spiritual Sonship, a complete and full heirship to all of the heavenly riches.

Our first concern is opening our consciousness to God. Our second concern is being sure that we are not going to a spiritual God asking for material things. We keep our prayer on the spiritual level:

> God, I seek Thy spiritual grace, Thy spiritual
> wholeness, Thy spiritual perfection, Thy spiritual
> harmony, Thy spiritual wisdom. I am not coming to
> Thee for loaves and fishes; I am not coming to
> Thee for bread; I am not coming to Thee for
> clothing or housing. I am coming to Thee only that
> Thou may enter into me and live my life,
> that I may be able to say with Paul,
> "I live; yet not I, but Christ liveth in me."

There is a spiritual kingdom. It is not of the earth, earthy; it is not known by man who has his being in the earth. It is known only to that man who has his being in Christ. There is a man of earth; there is a mortal man. He does not enter into the things of God; he does not enter into the joys, the blessings, or the abundance of God. Only those who are willing to make the transition, to seek that Christ, may enter in and experience the new man, the new birth, and the new world.

ACROSS THE DESK

In this world, we are constantly being presented with pictures of discord and inharmony. Joel has told us that our response to these appearances must be immediate, that is, we should see at once that they are suggestions, illusions, or hypnotism, and dismiss them. If this is our immediate reaction, we usually find that they disappear from our experience.

This sounds easy, but those of you who have worked with

this principle know how hard it is not to react to appearances. In fact, we face so many of these suggestions every day that, unless we are meditating and living in the atmosphere of Spirit constantly, many of these suggestions are hardly recognized and take root in our consciousness because of our lack of alertness.

To practice diligently nonreaction by recognizing error as nothingness is the way to be alert and aware that the only activity that is taking place is that of God.

Chapter Three

The Sword of the Spirit

Think not that I am come to send peace on earth:
I came not to send peace, but a sword.

Matthew 10:34

What a strange statement this is to come from a consciousness
such as that of the Master! Somehow or other we visualize
Jesus the Christ as sitting on cloud nine all the time, in peace, harmony, joy, and completeness, with no rainy days in between. Yet he
says, "I came not to send peace, but a sword."

A person may interpret this in any way he wishes, but I speak to
you about it from the standpoint of what I have witnessed in my
thirty-odd years in this work, and from my observation the reason
the Christ seems to bring a sword is that our purpose in life and the
Christ's purpose in life are two entirely different things.

In What Is Our Trust?

We think in terms of economic or physical good; we think of
peace, security, health, abundance, and happiness, but entirely in
human terms, always involving the acquisition of some materi-

al form of good to bring us that peace, harmony, wholeness, and completeness. Even nationally and internationally, we depend on a bomb for peace, a frightening concept of the condition required for peace, nevertheless a fact in this age. In the past we have depended on armaments to establish and maintain peace for our nation, and individually we have depended on sums of money or a measure of physical well-being. In our lifetime, however, we have witnessed the failure of all of these to give us peace, security, or happiness.

The Master, on the other hand, came to reveal a kingdom not of this world.[1] He came to reveal a peace also not of this world. His recipe for security was that we should not live by bread alone. Instead he gave us something to live by that to the ordinary human being seems almost impossible: the word of God. It seems strange to meet the threat of a bomb with the word of God, to meet the threat of disaster, famine, or disease with the word of God, and yet this is the Christ-ministry. We live not by "bread,"[2] by the world of effect, but by the word of God.

In the world of the Master's day, just as in our world today, force was the great power. Whether it was the force of arms, dollars, or material remedies, always it was force in one way or another, power of one kind or another, and yet the Master said, "Resist not evil.[3] . . . Put up . . . thy sword."[4]

Breaking Away from Human Reliances and Dependencies

The sword that the Master spoke of, the sword that he brought to us was actually the difficulty we have in giving up our faith and reliance on material means. This is the sword; this is the great trial and tribulation that we all go through. As a matter of fact, this is the problem that every individual who turns to the spiritual path faces.

I know that it is generally believed that if only we will turn to the spiritual path, life will be all sweetness and light. Most of us have already discovered that that is not so. When the spiritual path has been realized, it is, of course, sweetness and light; but until then we find the meaning of that sword: the breaking away from faith, hope, confidence, and reliance on external powers, whether those powers be of God, a prayer, a hymn, a rite, a ritual, a ceremony, or whatever it is that man has depended upon—armies, navies, or gold in the vault.

Until recently, the American dollar was all-powerful. When all the other currencies of the world were slipping, the American dollar stood fast. Why? We had twenty-two billion dollars of gold at Fort Knox. Today we have only a fraction of that, and when we read in the press that the dollar is threatened and that it has weakened, we now learn that it was not the gold that gave us a solid dollar: it was our national potential. Thinking in terms of anything as material as gold and silver, we find that even they are made up of ideas, labor, work, and all those things that could never be put in the nation's treasury.

So it is that, whether our dependence has been on gold, the Red, White, and Blue, or some other flag, or our dependence has been on some material thing, eventually this sword must come to our consciousness and sever from us all such hope, faith, and confidence, until we, individually and then collectively, begin to realize that man shall not live by bread alone— by form, by force, by power, by anything in the realm of effect—but rather man shall live "by every word that proceedeth out of the mouth of God."[5]

Giving Up Reliance On a God Without

The man of earth, the human being, really has no God to depend upon, no God from which he may derive this word of God. If he listens for it, he is probably looking toward heaven or back two thousand years ago to the shores of Galilee. Very seldom is he made to realize that if he is to listen for this "still small voice,"[6] if he is to listen for the word of God, he must do all his listening within himself.

According to the Master, "the kingdom of God is within you,"[7] but we have no way of knowing that, or knowing how much of his own realization Jesus divulged to his disciples about the nature of God. He may actually have revealed to them the secret of the nature of God, but it is not given in scripture in a way that is readily understandable. Therefore, in spite of these past four hundred years of the distribution of billions of copies of the Bible, the question is still asked, "What is God?"

To the extent that it is possible to answer such a question, it is answered in this message: God is consciousness, and that consciousness is the consciousness of the individual—of individual you and me. No one has ever yet taken a photograph of consciousness, and therefore we must accept the word "consciousness" as the intelligence, the substance, and the law of the universe, remembering always that we are speaking of God as the consciousness of individual you and me—not a consciousness out in space, not a consciousness in heaven or on a cross, but the consciousness that actually is functioning as our individual life and mind.

The Sword of the Prayer of Listening

When we can, in some way, feel the rightness of God as being closer to us than breathing, of God as consciousness, we will learn that prayer is actually a communion between me, my outer self, and *Me,* the divine consciousness of my being. These are one, not two, but insofar as all practical purposes are concerned, we are dealing with them as if they were two, as if there were a person whom the Master says can of his own self do nothing, and if he speaks of himself he bears witness to a lie. Then there is the same person, the *I* to which he can turn inwardly in communion, and by means of the listening ear draw forth the word of God, the Voice, which when It is uttered melts the entire universe of error.

Just as this sword of the Spirit must cut us loose from all faith, hope, and confidence in the external, even in a God; so, too, the sword very often cuts deeply into us when it is trying to turn us within, because if there is anything in the world that seems difficult to the human state of consciousness, it is to turn within and to be still. This is natural to the human race, because all of us have more or less been brought up right from infancy to play with rattles: rattles in one form or another to keep us engaged in the outer realm, almost as if it were a plot to keep us from having time enough to go within and listen and be at peace with the Spirit, with the Source of our existence, But this activity of listening is essential to progress on the path.

The Sword of Giving Up Turning Within for Material Things

The sword of the Spirit will function in our experience until we have been cut loose from all material reliances. About the time that we begin to realize that we must stop seeking in the external, that we must stop praying in the external and begin to go within, we may find ourselves trapped in the metaphysical idea of going within for new automobiles, new houses, new clothes, new marriages, or something of that kind, and we are once more turned off the track of spiritual demonstration, because just as we are about to learn to turn within, we learn also to turn within for the wrong things. In fact, we learn to go within for things, and of all mistakes, this is really the one big one. It would be better to continue seeking or praying to God up in heaven somewhere and praying for spiritual things than ever to have discovered the God within and keep seeking material things from that God.

"God is a Spirit: and they that worship him must worship him in spirit and in truth."[8] We take no thought for our life. Prayer is not a seeking of that which will feed, clothe, and house us: prayer must be a seeking of the kingdom of God, and since the kingdom of God is within us, that is where the seeking must be done.

It is surprising the rapid progress we make on the spiritual path the moment we stop turning to God, without or within, for any of the things of this world, and accept the truth that God is Spirit, that there is a kingdom of God, that it is entirely spiritual in nature, and that it can give us only the word of God. It has nothing else to give.

Heaven or Hell, a Question of Spiritual Discernment

When we receive the word of God, the earth melts. And what happens when the earth melts? Heaven is revealed, because actually that which we term the earth is heaven. Heaven, seen through three-dimensional eyes, is earth: the earth, seen through fourth dimensional eyes, is heaven. In other words, the very place whereon we stand is heaven. This is literally true, and when our senses testify that this place where we stand is hell—disease, sin, false appetite, death, poverty—then we may be assured that we are seeing through those eyes that have been accustomed to rattles, from baby rattles to atomic bomb rattles.

Yes, we have been rattling that atomic bomb, and it has been rattled at us, too. Nevertheless it is a rattle, a plaything of mankind, something to keep him occupied on the outer plane, something to divert his attention from the kingdom of God that is within, which is all-power, omnipotence. No, as long as we can be made to look at the mechanical power of the bomb, we never will believe that the word of God is more powerful than that bomb. But it is. So, too, those who have become spiritual healers have witnessed that the word of God is more powerful than the disease that is presented to them.

Wrestle with the Problem
Until the Consciousness of the Principle Is Attained

Jacob, wrestling with error all night, wrestled with nothing more nor less than the same sword of the Spirit, and when he recognized this truth, he did not stop wrestling with it until it had yielded up its blessings. So with us. Whether or not we like it, the particular sin, disease, lack, or limitation in our experience is going to persist, and we are going to have to continue wrestling with it until we learn to live by the word of God, the grace of God, the spiritual unfoldment from within.

We can carry most of our ills to our practitioners and teachers and sometimes receive great and complete healings, but we must not be fooled by that because tomorrow there will always be something else to plague us until we yield to the sword of the Spirit. I have never yet witnessed anyone in my years of healing experience healed of all the diseases he could contract, not until he awakened individually to the truth that health is not a condition of body any more than prosperity is a condition of money.

Health is a condition of consciousness: wealth is a condition of consciousness; security is a condition of consciousness; peace is a condition of consciousness. When we learn to turn to consciousness, our consciousness, the consciousness of individual you and me, and realize, "I have hidden manna.[9] . . . I have meat to eat that ye know not of,"[10] and realize that we have and that we are, then, in that higher consciousness we become aware of the word of God uttering Itself. Sometimes it is as the still small voice, and sometimes it thunders, but in one way or another we receive a spiritual impartation from within our own being.

Freedom Comes by Degrees
As the Principle Is Realized

A question often arises at this point: When we hear this Voice, when we receive an act of Grace, or when we receive an impartation of God, does it set us completely free from the problems of this world? The answer is, no. No one, including the Master, was ever set completely free from the problems of this world. In Paul's case it was called "a thorn in the flesh"[11]; in the Master's case it might have been called the Sanhedrin or Judas. But the name makes no difference. It is always the same thing: a universal belief in two powers which has not been overcome completely. It is always a belief in material security or material good of one nature or another, sometimes even a trust in people.

Whether or not the Master entirely trusted his disciples, we probably will never know. Certain it is that he must have been suspicious of one of them because later on he was able to name him quickly, so perhaps for some time prior to his tragic betrayal he had an idea of the nature of the "snake" that he was cherishing in his breast.

For our purpose, let us not think at this moment in terms of our ultimate freedom from this world; let us think rather in terms of the principle that will free us. In every case the principle reveals itself to us slowly, by degrees, in the measure of our capacity to understand it.

Some of us may remember the first airplane that crossed over the twenty-six miles of English Channel from France to England, and won twenty-five thousand pounds for doing it. Today we pay to make that journey: then they were paid for making it. But remember the nature of the planes in which they traveled. We could look at every mechanical product and go back and think of some of the older models and now at some of the new, such as the automobiles from the Model T's to today.

We can see how these principles revealed themselves to us in the degree of our ability to assimilate and grasp them.

So it is that we have very nearly completed a circle from the heights of revelation attained two thousand years ago to the very depths of religious ignorance, superstition, and paganism of only a century ago, and we have returned almost full circle to where we were two thousand years ago when it was revealed that *I* is God. Once more individuals here and there are hearing that Voice within them declare, "Be still, and know that I am God."[12] When they reach that place in consciousness, they have attained the heights that Moses, Isaiah, Buddha, and Jesus attained. They were at that state of consciousness where it was revealed to them that there is the kingdom of God within, and it voices itself in just that way:

Be still and know that *I* in the midst of you am God.
I will never leave you or forsake you;
I will be with you unto the end of the world.
I am the bread, the meat, the wine, the water,
the resurrection. *I* am life eternal.
I am come that you might have life,
and that you might have life more abundantly.

The Fruitage of Hearing the Voice Within

Think for one moment what will happen to us individually when we return to the silence within ourselves and let this Voice speak to us until we do hear: "*I* in the midst of thee am power. *I* in the midst of thee am the only power. Is there any other power but *Me?* Is there any other God but *Me?*"

When we receive this, and we can receive it very, very quickly if we can make up our mind in advance that when we do, we will not ask that *I* for a new automobile, a new home, a new dress, a new business, a new marriage, or a new anything else.

We will accept that *I* as omniscience, and realize that since It is the all-knowing, It already knows our needs, and it is Its good pleasure to give us the kingdom.

We must not try to translate the spiritual kingdom into terms of dollars, pounds, things, or thoughts, because God's thoughts are not our thoughts and God's ways are not our ways. God's grace is not something of a material nature; yet, when it appears, it comes to us in a tangible form that we call material good. The barrier is having some preconceived idea of what form it should take.

The sword of the Spirit must come to us to sever all our beliefs in some far-off God, sever all our theological beliefs about a God who gives or a God who withholds. All this must be taken from us. We will meet God face to face only when we hear the still small voice within us say that little word *I!*

> *I* am here. *I* am deathless. Neither life nor death
> can separate you from My love, for
> *I* am deathless; *I* am immortal; *I* am eternal.

We are God's own Selfhood expressed in an infinite individual way, but we must live, not by our human wisdom, not by our physical strength, not by our education, not by our bank account or our parents' bank account. We must learn to live by every Word that proceeds out of the mouth of God. Until this has been accomplished, that sword will continue to cut and cut and cut until it has cut away from us everything not necessary to the life of the son of God.

There Is No Sword
Once the Spiritual Life Is Attained

The spiritual life is not a difficult life. The spiritual life has no problems. It is only in the attaining of it that we find this sword. Once the spirit of God is upon us, once we are ordained unto that, life has very few problems, practically none of our own. Whatever problems touch us in life are only in the degree that we are still bearing the burdens of others. In some cases it could be family; in many cases it is our patients and our students who bring problems to us. But looking at our own life, we find very few problems because, once the spirit of the Lord God is upon us, we are free.

Our goal, then, is attaining that mind that was in Christ Jesus, attaining the ordination, attaining the ability to receive impartations from the Spirit within us, that we, too, may live by every Word that comes to us from within. Many have attained some measure of the spirit of God and live by It and are guided by It.

A Sufficiency of Grace for the Now

Attainment is made possible when we realize that God is our consciousness and that we need only turn constantly to our own consciousness, until it begins to utter itself to us and through us in tangible form. It does not come by effort: it comes by Grace. But there is an effort on our part, and that effort is, first of all, the knowing of the truth; that effort is coming into the awareness of the nature of God and the nature of prayer, so that we can more rightly pray.

We are told that if we pray and do not receive, it is that we pray amiss, and we know how true that is, because we do know that when prayer has attained some measure of rightness, tangible results come forth. Then what is righteous prayer? There can be no formula to encompass it, but we can understand that prayer is an inner communion, a communion within the individual which takes the form primarily of listening. Prayer also is this inner form of communion in which we are not seeking of God, but we are seeking only spiritual Grace, spiritual blessings, spiritual truth, the spiritual word. We have had seventeen hundred years of praying for things without getting them, and the least we can do now is to try to make our prayers entirely of a spiritual nature, entirely a seeking of the kingdom of God and the grace of God.

How often do we voice some statement such as, "Thy grace is my sufficiency in all things," and then turn around and think in terms of some form of material good! We have just said, "Thy grace is my sufficiency," and in the next moment Thy grace becomes what? A thing! But prayer really is the understanding that God's grace is our sufficiency in all things, and furthermore, there is always a sufficiency of God's grace present in our consciousness with which to meet the immediate needs.

Too often we think of God's grace meeting all our needs for the rest of our days, instead of being concerned with our needs for today. If we can think of ourselves as living today, and not only seeking the realization of God's grace, but realizing that there is a sufficiency of God's grace with which to meet today, each day then will take care of itself until yesterday and today and tomorrow all melt into each other.

Good Always Appears in the Now

We lay up treasures for the future, but these are for imaginary needs that we are going to have for the next ten years of so; whereas the only treasure that we need is the treasure of this moment, for this is always a continuing moment. The spiritual *now* is not like the now of time and space when we say "now," and then it is gone, but the spiritual *now* is an eternity, since spiritually it is always now, and we never get past now. Now never fades into the past; now never becomes the future.

The spiritual now is an infinity and an eternality of this very moment, and if only we could seek the realization of God's grace in the now as a sufficiency unto this moment of now, we also would discover that having attained it now, it never leaves us or forsakes us, because now never disappears; it is always the same now in which our good appears.

One of the fallacies of the old metaphysical practice was seeking a demonstration of supply this year, and perhaps making it, and then seeking another demonstration of supply next year, as if a spiritual demonstration had to be made twice. We lose the evidence of our demonstration by believing that it was an event of the past, instead of an activity of the Spirit.

The Nature of Spiritual Demonstration

One of these days it will be realized that when we have a healing spiritually we will be healed forever, because certainly a spiritual activity does not have to take place twice. A spiritual activity must partake of eternality and infinity. Therefore, a spiritual demonstration once realized should be a permanent one, and will be, when we realize that the demonstration was not the demonstration of supply, and it was not the demonstration of a healing: it was a demonstration of the omnipotence and omnipresence and omniscience of God. That is the demonstration that is made when a spiritual demonstration is made. It is never a demonstration of things.

We cannot demonstrate an automobile spiritually; we cannot demonstrate a home; we can only demonstrate that God is omniscience, omnipotence, and omnipresence, and when we have demonstrated that, we have demonstrated it for all time in all degrees.

Our demonstration is the demonstration of God's grace. It need be made only once in our experience. Our demonstration is the realization of Christ as our true identity, and this demonstration need be made only once. Our demonstration is that we live by the word of God, and this demonstration need be made only once.

The Nagging of the Sword of the Spirit

Probably one reason that makes me say so often that I have not fully attained is that the sword of the Spirit keeps nagging, never letting me rest for fear that I might believe sometime that I have fully attained and then miss the way. Like Jacob, I am going to say, "No, I am going to wrestle with it. I am going to stay right with these problems until this spirit of God is so clearly realized that freedom then becomes the full and complete demonstration of Christhood."

Is it clear why the sword of the Spirit plagues us? We have so many beliefs that must be specifically removed from our thought, from our mind, from our beliefs; and that sword of the Spirit is really the surgeon's knife. How else except by this prodding, this continual nagging of the sword of the Spirit will we ever relinquish our finite beliefs, concepts, opinions, theories, and theologies? How else?

ACROSS THE DESK

The purpose of our work is the demonstration of God— not the seeking of things. It is important to read and study the writings and, when they are available to students, to listen to the tape recordings. All this provides the foundation with which to build our spiritual house of consciousness and keeps us from falling into the pitfalls sincere aspirants on the path may encounter.

But God cannot be demonstrated with a book: God can be realized, demonstrated, only by turning to where God may be found: within. Until we go on to that further step of meditation, the reading, the studying, and the listening will remain only words. Through meditation, the words take on new meaning and are illumined by the light of that Spirit within.

Students cannot be urged too strongly to incorporate meditation into their day's program. This is an activity of such great significance that no matter what else is omitted, frequent brief periods of meditation should be a regular part of their daily schedule, as well as time set aside for longer periods of contemplation and listening. A hit or miss program will not bring about that deeper awareness which students are all seeking. So be diligent and persistent in this practice, and realization will be your reward. It may require great effort in the early stages, but the fruitage is well worth the effort.

TAPE RECORDED EXCERPTS
Prepared by the Editor

For most persons, God exists for the one purpose of giving them more and better things and persons of this world. All their prayers to this concept of God are directed toward that end. Those who embark on the spiritual path, however, find that the sword of the Spirit will not permit them to continue in this attempt to make God do their will. The sword of the Spirit cuts them loose from the moorings of desire, but only that desire might be replaced by fulfillment, and the freedom and expansiveness of Christ-consciousness take over their life. The excerpts from the tape recordings given below make so clear the importance of this activity of the sword of the Spirit that they are included in this month's letter.

The Sword of Desirelessness

"To begin with, we are not seeking things or persons. That is not our function on the spiritual path. It was a step in the right direction when we learned to turn from material and mental efforts towards a spiritual consciousness for the solution of our human problems. But that step leads us now to a place where we realize that human problems only disappear in proportion as we attain that mind which was also in Christ Jesus, as we attain that actual consciousness of oneness with God.

"Any desire for things or persons will prevent or delay our entrance into the spiritual kingdom; whereas with the constant reminder within ourselves that the goal we are seeking is God-contact, God-realization, Self-realization, . . . we find all things added unto us or we find all things included. . . .

"We must develop the habit, first of all, of realizing that we have no goal other than the achievement of the kingdom of God, that we have no demonstration to make except the demonstration of our spiritual selfhood.

"What is the best way, if there is a best way, to achieve this realization of our true selfhood? Is there a shortcut? Is there a path that leads to God-realization, a path that can be trod here on earth without waiting for the hereafter, or that can be brought into realization in time? And the answer is: Yes, not only are there ways of achieving it here on earth, but there is a shortcut. That shortcut is to perform a bit of mental surgery on ourselves and cut out all our desires. That is the shortcut. Take a good sharp knife and cut right out of ourselves, right out of the heart and soul and mind, all desire for person, place, thing, circumstance, or condition—even all desire to save the world, all desire to benefit mankind, all desire to bring peace on earth. Every desire must be cut out in order that only one remains. That is the shortcut, when we have only one desire: to know Thee aright."

Joel S. Goldsmith, "The Realized Christ,"
The 1955 First Kailua Study Group.

"Give up the desire for health, for supply, for goodness, for home, for companionship, and rest in the fact that God is a state of Self-completeness, of Self-fulfillment, God is the only good whether that good is a goodly supply of wherewithal or whether it is a good supply of health. God is the only good. God does not acquire it or achieve it or attain it: God is it. . . .

"Do not add more fish, bigger fish, or better fish to your nets. Deny that you have any need of fish because all the fish in the sea belong to God, and in the back of your mind you know that anything that belongs to God belongs to you. Why? Because 'I and my Father are one.' There is no point of transfer between that which is in God and that which is in you. All that is in God is in you at this very moment."

Joel S. Goldsmith, "Deny Thyself; Die Daily; How?"
The 1955 First Kailua Study Group.

"You release God completely and realize: God, never again will I try to make You do something for me or seek that You do something for me or will that You do something for me. Now I know that it lies within me to yield myself to Thee. Now I realize that it lies within me to mold my will to God's will. God is; God is functioning; and if I am not benefitting by the will of God, the way of God, the acts of God, it is because I have in some way removed myself from that way, that will. . . .

"It is not as difficult as it seems. The difficulty presents itself to us in the beginning when we are called upon to relinquish all our concepts of God and prayer, when we are called upon to stop praying to God for something, when we are called upon to stop praying for somebody, when we are compelled to leave ourselves almost in a vacuum, without God, until realization begins to dawn. There is, of course, that difficult period when we would still cling to the God whom we ignorantly worship, the mythical God, the fictional God, when we would still cling to praying to that God for something for us or for our mother or for our child, as if, heaven forbid, God could single any one of us out for a favor.

"We were born that God's will may be done on earth, that

God's way may be manifest on earth, that God's glory may be evidenced on earth. This can never come about while we are trying to fulfill ourselves, separate and apart from God, but only when we relinquish ourselves that His will may be done in us, His glory may be expressed through us, His heaven may be made manifest on earth through us."

Joel S. Goldsmith, "Molding Our Lives to God,"
The 1962 Hawaiian Village Open Class.

Chapter Four

Life Unfolding As the Fruitage of Attained Consciousness

Every person is the product of what he accepts in consciousness. Watch this operate, and watch it well. Watch it carefully, because it can mark a turning point in the experience of everyone. Even those who, it would seem, are the most advanced must begin anew every day, because no one stores up enough truth from yesterday to carry him forward into tomorrow. Each one has to open his consciousness day by day that the fresh manna, the fresh inspiration, may fall.

God is infinite. But how could anyone in his present experience even begin to grasp the tiniest part of Infinity? Is it not clear that for everyone there is something deeper and richer, something truer that unfolds today, something that enriches his consciousness today and becomes greater fruitage tomorrow?

In a Moment of Loving, Love Wipes Out Negative Qualities

When you are in a room that is filled with love, such as an Infinite Way class, your whole consciousness becomes imbued with that love. You look up at the teacher with love in your heart, mind, and soul, with understanding and gratitude, and you know that the teacher is responding to that, loving every moment and loving every individual who has shown enough interest in the spiritual path to be there. Under such circumstances, at that minute, your consciousness is filled with love and so is that of the teacher.

Suppose that this love that you feel at that moment could be a continuing experience? Suppose you keep on feeling love, only not necessarily for the teacher, because the teacher may be somewhere else, but you will still be loving. You will be loving whoever it is that is there, or whoever it is that you meet elsewhere, because love has now been established in your consciousness.

In that continuing moment of loving, the past is gone; and the proof is that regardless of how much hate, malice, resentment, jealousy, or of how many negative qualities of any nature you may have felt in the past, these are now absent from you. Nothing is present with you now but love. Therefore, in your consciousness, there is no past: there is only this moment of love.

Although your clocks are marked off by little periods called seconds, minutes, and hours, if all the clocks were to be removed from the world, would there be any marks of any kind anywhere in the universe indicating a past or a future? Are you not always in reality living in the consciousness of now? Life can be lived only in the now, and so whatever life you are living in the now is the only life that you possess, and that life in a continuing moment of loving is love.

The Love of Truth Received in a Moment of Now Becomes a Continuing Experience

Since time does not end and since love does not end, do you not see that the love that you were feeling in that class-experience was not love for a person? The love that you felt is the love for God, the love for truth. You are not loving a person: you are loving the truth that has been voiced. Did you stop loving truth when you walked out of that love-filled room? No, you are on this path. Nothing will ever take you from this path, and therefore, the love of truth which you felt is a continuing experience throughout all your days within this parenthesis, within this span of life.

Every word of truth that you have ever accepted in consciousness from the first day of your entering the pathway of truth is stored up in you now, because when you received it, it was now, and now is a continuing experience, and the truth within you has perpetuated itself in the now. This truth will be abiding with you until the end of this parenthesis.

Think of this: *I* will be with you. Truth will be with you; the spiritual Christ will be with you unto the end of this world, unto the end of this parenthesis, this life span.

Life, a Parenthesis in the Circle of Eternity

Life has been depicted as a circle, and one of the ancient mystics has written that a person's present human life is a parenthesis in that circle, just a small part of the whole, and that he knew life before he was born into this life-experience. Because it is a circle, he must have pre-existed from the very beginning, and because it is a circle, there will never be an end. What is called birth and death represent the two parts of the parenthesis. By removing one, the flow from the past into the present is noted; by removing the other, the continuity of life, flowing beyond this parenthesis right around the circle, is revealed.

The truth that you have lived eternally and will live eternally enables you to understand the reason for the discord, the inharmony, the lack and limitation, and the harmony, the benefits and the fruitage that you experience during this particular parenthesis.

Memory, the Only Substance of the Past

From this, you can see how simple it is for those who are willing to do so to wipe out the past and begin a new today and a fresh tomorrow. To begin with, there is no such thing as a past or a future.

The only thing you can ever know of what is called the past is what you can draw up in memory or draw forth from someone else's memory. No one can know the future, because, regardless of what the stars report or what the lines of your palms may indicate, regardless of what your karma may be thought to be—whether your sins have been scarlet, or whether you have been the woman taken in adultery or the thief on the cross—regardless of how much karma you have stored up, you can dispense with it at any moment of your life and witness that it cannot go forward even into the next minute without your bringing it there through memory.

Ignorance Is Wiped Out in a Moment of Awareness

The truth is that we are consciousness, states and stages of consciousness, with some further advanced along the path than others, but we are all consciousness. In our original true being, we are divine Consciousness. That divine Consciousness is the reality of our being, and any limitation or discord, any sin or disease is no part of our consciousness, but is a superimposed picture.

Consciousness, Itself, always remains pure, and that is why at any moment of the day or night of this year or any year, you can remove the dust and grime that may have found lodgment in your state of consciousness, and start out in any moment pure, white as snow, regardless of how deep the red may have been.

In that atmosphere of love and truth you experienced, your

ignorance of life and truth could not and cannot enter in. When the Master says, "Father, forgive them; for they know not what they do,"[1] he is saying that a person sins only because of his ignorance of truth, his ignorance of his spiritual identity. Remember that this wisdom, which you have attained in your years on this path—this truth and this love—is the light of your life, and in this light there is no ignorance.

In that moment of awareness, the ignorance under which you lived in the past has been eliminated, and you are now the embodiment of the love, the life, and the truth which you are experiencing in this continuing minute.

Let me repeat that: Every bit of love, life, and truth that you felt in a moment of heightened awareness is what you are embodying, and it constitutes your being, and this is you. Light, love, life, truth: these are you; these are your present state of consciousness. How then can the past intrude into the present? How can darkness enter light?

Planting the Seeds of Truth

As you maintain in your consciousness the realization that truth has embodied itself within you—light, life, love—this is your continuing experience. At this point, a miracle takes place. You have read in scripture: "Whatsoever a man soweth, that shall he also reap. For he that soweth to his flesh shall of the flesh reap corruption; but he that soweth to the Spirit shall of the Spirit reap life everlasting."[2]

Ever since you have been on the pathway of truth, have you not been sowing to the Spirit? Ever since you began to read a truth-book, have you not been sowing to the Spirit? Every time you have attended a lecture or a class on spiritual wisdom, have you not been sowing to the Spirit? Every time you have read and every time you have meditated, have you not been sowing to the Spirit? What else have you been doing these years except sowing to the Spirit? And how can scripture lie? You have been sowing to the Spirit, and you are reaping life everlasting.

This is not a future event; you are not storing up for a future life, for life can be lived only in the now. No one has ever lived yesterday, and no one has the power to live five minutes from now. The only life you will ever know is the life that you are living now, and in this now you are sowing to the Spirit; you are planting within yourself seeds of truth, and the harvest must be life harmonious, life eternal.

Surmounting Karma

Since you have learned that you reap what you sow, and since you have been sowing to the Spirit, you have been preparing for the harvest which has to come in its due season: the harvest of harmony, peace, abundance, and spiritual grace. If you who are reading this letter have not been on the spiritual path up to now or have not been sowing to the Spirit, let me say that the sowing can begin at any moment of your choosing. You can choose now what you will serve: sowing to the flesh or sowing to the Spirit. By agreeing to sow to the Spirit, you wipe out karma; you wipe out the penalty of former wrongdoing, wrong thinking, or wrong acting.

In the ancient Oriental teachings, the karma that you sowed, especially the bad karma, remained with you for many, many lifetimes, until heaven knows what it took finally to erase it. Of course, that never was true. That was merely a concept of some writer or teacher, but the Christian era disposed of that and revealed what is now demonstrable, and that is that all your evil karma, all your former wrong thinking or wrongdoing is wiped out in a moment of repentance—not in years of working it out, not in years of suffering, not in years between heaven and hell, and not in years of paying a penalty on earth. No!

In my own experience, a moment after the first light, the

entire past with its desires and its punishments dropped away. I have witnessed in the years that have followed how many students, in coming to a place of actual repentance for any of their previous wrongs—some of omission, some of commission, some serious, some not so serious—have, in that moment of accepting the spiritual path, wiped out the past, and with their sowing to the Spirit, with their sowing to truth, they have begun very quickly to reap spiritual harmony, spiritual peace, an inner awareness of forgiveness, and an inner awareness of release from the burdens of the human sense of life.

I speak not only of sin in terms of what the world calls sin, but also of disease, lack, or limitation, all of which are really sins from the standpoint of spiritual living because they miss the mark of spiritual perfection. Your diseases are as readily wiped out as your sins; your lack and limitation are wiped out as readily as your sins—but only in one way: by sowing to the Spirit, by sowing to truth, by pondering the word of God, by taking the word of God into consciousness, by meditating and contemplating on the word of God. In that moment, you are sowing to the Spirit, you are sowing to truth; and it will not be long before you will be reaping spiritual fruitage, spiritual harmony, spiritual health, spiritual supply, spiritual companionship, and witnessing all these translated into terms of human harmony.

Sowing Now Brings Forth Reaping Now

This sowing to the Spirit must take place in the now. There must be a moment of nowness in which you acknowledge: I have turned from darkness to the light; I have turned from the past to the present; I have turned from ignorance to understanding. Even though I may not wake up tomorrow morning and find myself to be a perfect human being, and certainly will not find wings sprouting, nevertheless, in this now of my acceptance of spiritual sowing, I immediately begin the process of reaping. The crop that I am to reap has begun. It began when I began sowing the seed.

The moment the seed is sown, it begins to work, and nature begins to work in it, and in due time the sprouts appear, and then the reaping. But remember, it all begins with a certain moment. Scriptural language calls it repentance. "I have no pleasure in the death of him that dieth, saith the Lord God: wherefore turn yourselves, and live ye."³ It has to do with a moment of repentance, a moment of turning from sowing to the flesh, a moment of turning from putting your faith in matter and in the externals and baubles of life, to realizing that everything that exists in the external is but the externalization of something that exists in consciousness.

Choose Now What You Will Sow

If you have truth abiding in your consciousness, you are manifesting or externalizing the fruitage of truth, which is life harmonious, life joyous, life abundant, life everlasting. If you are filling your consciousness with a faith in the externals and the baubles of life, then of course you are sowing to the flesh, and you must reap corruption. In either case, you have to do it now; you have to do your sowing now.

"Choose you this day whom ye will serve."⁴ In this moment when your heart and soul are filled with love—love for truth, love for God, love for your spiritual teacher, love for the Christ, love for every mystic who has ever given us a golden thread of truth to weave into that great consciousness, the great fabric of life eternal—as your heart is filled with this love, with this gratitude, realize that in that very love, in that very recognition of truth, you are sowing to the Spirit.

Every time that you open a book of spiritual wisdom, every time you attend a spiritual lecture or class, you are sowing to the Spirit anew, and reaping still more tomorrows of spiritual harmony and spiritual realization. It is for this reason that no matter how ardent your love for truth is in this moment, remember that when you awaken tomorrow, it will still be now, and every moment of tomorrow you will be sowing. Therefore, remember the sowing of this moment, and continue your sowing tomorrow by loving truth, by taking into your consciousness the word of truth, by filling yourself with truth on every occasion, and thereby store up still richer reaping for the now that comes the next day.

The now of this moment is still the now of tomorrow morning. It is now extending itself, but it is always now. Every moment in which you think is a moment of now; every moment in which you live is a moment of now. So you are sowing in every moment, and at the same time, you are reaping the sowing of now, the now that is *now*.

Not Death but Transition

You may have experienced in your life either regret that you did not accept more education when you had the opportunity to receive it, or you may be experiencing great joy because you did accept the opportunity to receive education when it was given you. If you did not accept education, you may have experienced some hardships since then that might have been avoided, or you may not be in quite the position in life you would be had you accepted that education. If you did avail yourself of the opportunity for education, you are probably now in a better position in life because of that acceptance. In other words, what you sowed in the area of education, you are reaping now in a more abundant life.

This same truth applies to your spiritual development after you leave this plane of life. For all of you, there will come a day when this parenthesis is removed, and you will pass from this experience into another. For those uninstructed in truth, it is called death. Actually it never is death, and for those instructed in truth, it is not even a claim of death: it is really a transition from one experience into another. It is very much like growing out of childhood into early maturity, and then growing out of that early maturity into the later years of maturity without having to die to do it. It is a gradual evolutionary process, a transitional experience. Eventually the day will come when you will leave this scene. Those on the spiritual path will accomplish this when their task has been completed, and not before.

Can you know what your experience will be? The answer is yes. The sowing that you do today will be the reaping you do then. The higher you go in spiritual understanding, the deeper and richer the spiritual consciousness that you attain here, the deeper and richer the consciousness that you will have as yours there.

Jesus' Preparation

Consider the Master, Christ Jesus. The truth of his preparation for his ministry is being revealed in the Dead Sea Scrolls and other writings. It is believed that the Master was in an Essene monastery from the time he was twelve until he was thirty and, along with his cousin, he learned the laws and the teachings of the Essene movement.

When he left the monastery, he began his preaching or rabbinical career, because he was ordained a rabbi in the Essene movement, a movement unpopular in those days because of its great austerity. It was based on highly spiritual teachings rather than on ceremonies, rites, and rituals of religious worship. This you can gather from the fact that the Master continuously reminded the people that God had no pleasure in their sacrifices and that God is not to be found in a holy temple. Certainly he overthrew the money changers' tables and the selling of doves to show that the church method was wrong and that the spiritual way was right.

By the life and mission of the Master, by his healing works, and by his exaltation into the consciousness of Reality, we know that he was probably the deepest and richest spiritual consciousness ever to walk the earth, and if not the greatest, at least one of the greatest.

What Becomes of an Enriched and Ripe Consciousness?

What do you think happened to that rich, ripe consciousness after the crucifixion, the burial, the resurrection, the ascension? What do you think happened to that consciousness? The answer was given at the tomb: "He is risen."[5] You cannot entomb a consciousness. Consciousness is not material: consciousness is incorporeal. Consciousness is not in your body: consciousness governs your body. Therefore, if some part of the body is taken away, you still have consciousness. Eventually the entire body may be taken away, but you still would have consciousness, because your consciousness never was in that body. No surgeon has ever found consciousness entombed in a body, no matter on what part of the body he has operated. It is not there; it was not there; it cannot be there. As a matter of fact, your consciousness is not even confined to the room in which you are sitting. It is for this reason that you can travel the globe while sitting in your own home because you are not confined to a body or a place.

When you leave your body somewhere, you will find that your consciousness goes on, and the consciousness that was the mind that was in Christ Jesus, that consciousness which God gave to man, has never been withdrawn from man. It is not dead: it lives!

The consciousness of Jesus Christ, having evolved to the extent that it did, still lives at that level of consciousness, or if possible, at an even higher level. I bring this to your attention so that you will know that whatever measure of attained spiritual consciousness you reach on this plane of life, because of your present sowing to the Spirit and to truth, is the measure that will accompany you into your next experience around that circle of life.

The Present Experience, the Fruitage of Attained Consciousness

If you attain a consciousness of peace, of health, of freedom, a consciousness of joy and of abundance, you will not be born into slavery, ignorance, toil, or hardship. The consciousness that you attain and demonstrate here is the consciousness that you attain and demonstrate here is the consciousness that you will experience there.

The question has often been asked: Why is it that some persons are born in countries where there is freedom or come to them later? What is there about such persons that entitled them to this great freedom, prosperity, joy, and abundance, and does not provide it for those who still live in the slave countries, the poverty-stricken countries, or the countries that are held in spiritual ignorance?

If you have ever been inclined to believe that life is unjust, lose that belief right now. No one can externalize any state of consciousness he has not attained. Those who are free have attained the consciousness of freedom, and they are externalizing it. Those who are experiencing abundance have attained the consciousness of abundance, and they are externalizing it. Those who have attained the consciousness of health are healthy, and they are externalizing their consciousness of health. They are reaping what they have sown.

At some time, whether in a previous existence or in your existence here on this plane since your birth, somewhere, sometime, you have sown to the Spirit; you have sown to the truth to a sufficient degree to give you whatever measure of harmony, peace, freedom, or joy you are now having. This must forever be the signal to you that you never will have more of anything, except in proportion to your more sowing to the Spirit, to Truth. Then, and then only, will there be a reaping of spiritual harmony, wholeness, perfection, and completeness.

The Master spoke from the standpoint of *now,* and he also taught from the standpoint of *you.* "Ye shall know the truth, and the truth shall make you free."[6] You shall live in the Word and let the Word live in you, and you will reap greater spiritual fruitage. You must forgive seventy times seven; you must forgive your enemies, pray for your enemies. You! The whole of the Master's ministry deals with you, showing you that as you sow to the Spirit, as you sow to truth, only in that proportion do you enter *My* kingdom, the Christ-kingdom. Always it is *you,* and *always it is now.*

Life Gives Back Only What Has Been Put into It

Be assured, you could not possibly accept the truth that is presented in this letter unless you had been preparing yourself, that is, sowing to the Spirit. This means that whatever degree of harmony you now have, you are having because you are reaping what you have sown. By this, know that whatever measure of love you feel now—love for truth, love for God, love for Christ, love for spiritual reality, love for spiritual things—whatever measure of life is tingling in your veins now, whatever of joy and of gratitude is within you now, this is your sowing to Truth, to the Spirit, and this is the measure of your reaping in the now which may appear tomorrow, next week, next month, or next year. At that moment it will be now, and it will be at that moment when the fruitage will appear in your experience, the fruitage of the seed sown now.

This is the essential characteristic of the mystical life and of the life of every mystic who has realized that the spirit of God at some moment of now entered his soul and inspired him with the desire for truth, a love for truth, a seeking for truth; and as he followed it, he came, not only to those periods of continued sowing, but eventually to the moments of reaping.

From now to the end of your parenthesis on this plane, remember that you will be reaping the fruitage of the seeds you are now sowing. There is no past. When you come to the end of this particular span, the seeds of truth that have taken root in your consciousness, the days and years of dedication to truth that you have given to this life are the measure of your reaping now and in every life to come. No one takes from life what he does not put into it. No one can demonstrate anything in life but the state of his own consciousness. If, by some freak of human circumstance, you get more than your share temporarily, it is impossible to hold it permanently. You can hold only that which is a part of your very own consciousness. In the degree, and to the extent, that you increase your sowing to the Spirit, will you increase your reaping of spiritual Grace.

Across the Desk

Easter brings us the message of life eternal and, through the focusing of attention on the experience of the Master Christ Jesus, reveals its continuity and eternality. Let us not, however, wait until the Easter season to remember this great truth.

As part of our preparation for the day, we should realize the nature of life: its on-goingness and foreverness. The understanding of God as life negates any possibility of an aging process. That life which is God is ageless, knowing no such thing as birth, maturity, or deterioration with its attendant depletion of faculties.

Life *is*. The invisible life, the forms of which we see, forever is. And this is the message of Easter. Let us be living witnesses to that great message of life eternal.

TAPE RECORDED EXCERPTS
Prepared by the Editor

To those of us on the spiritual path, the events the Christian world commemorates as Christmas, Maundy Thursday, Good Friday, and Easter are individual experiences in consciousness which mark stages in our progress on the spiritual path. Christmas is perhaps the most joyous of all these; Easter, the most glorious and triumphant; and Good Friday the most dismal and the saddest. If, however, we could see Good Friday in its proper perspective as a necessary and forward step on the path, it would lose much of its gloom.

Good Friday, the crucifixion of personal sense, must come to everyone before there can be an Easter, before there can be a rising out of the dark tomb of personal sense. How difficult and how severe is our experience of Good Friday depends upon the tenacity with which we hold on to personal sense. Seen in its real light, Good Friday is that glorious day of giving up the false sense of personal selfhood for the reality of divine sonship. Joel gives this principle special emphasis in the following excerpts from the tape recordings.

Good Friday

"Spiritually speaking, we do not celebrate the death of Jesus. . . nor. . . the resurrection of Jesus as a physical form, for then we would be limited to basking in the reflected glory of something someone else did but which we know right well we cannot do. The purpose of the lesson of the death of Jesus and his resurrection, since he is the wayshower, is to show us the way to find life eternal.

"That way is by means of the death of personal sense. We, too, are supposed to die to our personal sense of life and to be resurrected from that tomb. In other words, our personal sense of life is a tomb in which we are buried. We have to die to the belief that we are something, that we have a life of our own, a mind of our own, a soul of our own, a way and a will of our own. We are supposed to die to the belief that we have possessions of our own or any virtue or any life, any being, any harmony, or any success of our own.

"In the resurrection, we come to the realization that there is that within us that can rise out of the tomb of personal sense and walk this earth as a spiritual being: God-fed, God-directed, God-wise, God-maintained, God-sustained. In celebrating these two events, our spiritual interpretation of them really does not permit us to memorialize them.

"Good Friday is a day in which we should contemplate and meditate upon its inner meaning. We can use the Master Christ Jesus as a symbol or as a wayshower. Go back to the four Gospels and reconstruct in thought his life, his ministry, his death, and his resurrection, and thereby find how he brought about the death of personal sense and how he avoided having problems, even when he had the serious problem of being faced with betrayal and death, how by not considering it a personal affliction or a personal problem he was able to rise above it: 'To this end was I born'—therefore, this is not a problem. . . .

"It makes no difference what it is, Jesus had it to share, yet always reminding you, 'I can of mine own self do nothing. If I speak of myself, I bear witness to a lie. . . . . Why callest thou me good?' And then you see the principle of Good Friday, the principle of the crucifixion of personal selfhood, personal sense, a crucifixion of the belief that we of ourselves have qualities of good or quantities of good. Then comes the resurrection in the realization: I am nothing, but I can give you all. . . .

"What we really have is another day for contemplation of another spiritual principle of life. . . the principle of self-renunciation, the principle of crucifixion, the principle of self-abnegation, in which, when we have brought to light the nothingness of our human selfhood, we then reveal the allness and immortality and eternality of our being."

Joel S. Goldsmith, "Maundy Thursday, Good Friday, Easter: Esoteric Meaning," *The 1959 Maui Advanced Work.*

"In all of us there remains a finite sense of self which, in the last analysis, must be crucified. Moses had it in that feeling of his unworthiness; Jesus had it for a great while in his feeling of 'I can of mine own self do nothing.' . . . Each of you has it in the measure that you believe you have a skill, wisdom, or a talent. . . . In the degree that you believe you have it, ultimately that will have to be crucified until in the end you can realize, 'I do not have any truth of my own; I do not know any truth; I do not have any skill of my own; I do not have any talent of my own: *I* am the truth; *I* am the talent; *I* am the skill. In that moment, humanhood has 'died,' and Christhood has been born in Its fullness and revealed in Its fullness, and the ascension or translation can take place.

"It is the personal sense of 'I' that must 'die,' the personal sense of 'I' that must be crucified."

Joel S. Goldsmith, "Truth Unveiled,"
The 1963 Kailua Private Class.

Chapter Five

Putting Off the Old Man
and Rebirth

The purpose of a work such as the Infinite Way is to die to the "old man,"[1] and to be reborn of the Spirit: not partially reborn, but wholly reborn, putting on a whole new consciousness, a whole new mind, that "mind. . . which was also in Christ Jesus."[2]

In the practical working out of this, the realization of the fullness of this Christ-consciousness may not be attained in a moment. That is because the Christ-consciousness is not attained through the acquiring of knowledge, not even acquiring a knowledge of truth. A person could know all the truth that has ever been revealed in all the philosophies and all the mystical writings known to man and still not have one single touch of Christ-consciousness.

The Vessel Must Be Emptied of Self

It is not any degree of human wisdom or any degree of human goodness that we may attain that brings forth the Christ. In fact, it might be far easier for some deep-dyed sinner to attain the Christ than for some very good person. The sinner is often well aware of his unworthiness. In his attitude of being "one of the least of these,"[3] and understanding his own inadequacy, he has so emptied himself that he is ready to be filled with the Christ; whereas, as a rule, if a person is living a fairly good human life, he is likely to get the idea, "Hmm! I am good; I deserve to have this blessing. I really have worked hard for it and I deserve it." It does not come that way; it comes by Grace, and that Grace can come only in proportion as a person is emptied so that there is no self left to be good.

As long as a person has a trace of a belief that he is good, deserving, or worthy, in that degree he is setting up a barrier for the entrance of the Christ. The Christ does not come while a vessel is already full of self and of a human being's goodness. The Christ comes when a person is so emptied of self that he has renounced not only the evil but also the good and has thus made himself completely empty so that when anyone says to him, "How good you are! How benevolent you are! How kind you are! How loving you are!" his response quite automatically is, "Why do you call me good? You know right well that this is the spirit of God working through me."

Has Our Particular Temptation Come to Us?

It is folly for anyone to claim any wisdom, charitableness, morality, or integrity, as if such qualities were of himself. In most cases, it is not possible to know whether a person would have such qualities if and when the temptation to which he is vulnerable came along. Different people succumb to different temptations; they do not yield to just any temptation that presents itself. It has to be *the* one. Somebody said that every man has his price, and it is only necessary to find what that price is. A few years ago, in a widely publicized medical report, it was found that most persons commit adultery at least once in their life. That may not be true of everyone, but according to the findings of this report, it is true of a great many people. Even if they have not been thus tempted, most persons are in no position to say that there is no form of temptation that could not, if it came at the right moment, prove to be too much to resist.

It behooves nobody to believe that his goodness is his own. If a person has reached a point where he knows that he is absolutely above any possibility of yielding to any temptation, then he must also know that it is not because of himself but because of something greater than himself that functions within him.

Putting Off the Old Consciousness

From the moment that we first opened a book of truth, regardless of what school of truth it was, and from the moment we first started reading, the old man began to die, and the rebirth of the new man had begun. The old consciousness began to disappear, and the new consciousness was beginning to appear. It came so gradually that at first it was not noticeable. For a long time we could not see that any change had taken place, but one day somebody said, "Oh, isn't the weather terrible? You are bound to catch cold now," and automatically our thought jumped back with, "Why? Why?" That was evidence that we had already caught a glimpse that the power is not outside in a germ, in the weather, or in the climate, and in that degree, the new consciousness had been born.

In one way or another, as an appearance of error made itself evident in our experience, we were able to say, "No, it does not have power"; or, "It is not power"; or, "It does not have jurisdiction over me." That was our new consciousness talking, not the old, because the old consciousness was fearful of everything from the tiniest germ up to the biggest bomb. But as the new consciousness developed, we automatically rejected every suggestion of power in form or effect, or of a power apart from God.

One day the appearance of an evil person came our way, and we realized, "No, no man is evil. Evil is an impersonal thing. Every man is born of God." That statement came forth from our new consciousness, not from the old, because the old one was always judging, criticizing, and condemning. As we go along in the development of our new consciousness, we can later watch our progress by the degree in which we no longer fear anything in the external world, and the degree in which we no longer judge, criticize, or condemn anything or any person in the external world.

How Much Time Are We Devoting to the Building of the New Consciousness?

Part of the process of dying daily and of being reborn is really the process of taking spiritual truths into consciousness. Every time that we add some spiritual truth to our awareness, we have increased the stature of the new man and decreased that of the old man. We may still see no effects outwardly because the whole experience is cumulative. If for a year we give one hour a day to truth—to reading, meditating, and practicing— we are going to find in the next year some measure of either greater harmony or less discord. If we give four hours each day for a year, we are going to find in our second year that much more of harmony and that much less of discord.

The amount of time and effort we give to truth determines the degree of harmony we enjoy next year. So also, the time and effort that we do not give to truth determines the amount of discord that can come into our experience next year. We are building our experience every day of our life. "Whatsoever a man soweth, that shall he also reap."[4] As a man soweth *when?* As he sows this minute. Now is the time. Let us not talk about the past; let us not talk about the future. We are interested only in one time, and that time is now, and it is now that we are building our tomorrows, our next years, and all the succeeding years. With what is going on in our consciousness now, we are determining our future. There is no use for anyone to wish us a good year if we are not building that good year now.

Transferring Power from the Outer to the Inner

Centuries ago, it was taught that "he that soweth to his flesh shall of the flesh reap corruption."[5] What does sowing to the flesh mean? It means that if we make our body the end and aim of existence, if we give power to form, if we give power to material sense, if we rely on material good, we are sowing to the flesh.

We are sowing to the Spirit only in the degree that we are transferring power from the outer realm to the inner, in the degree in which we realize: "No, my consciousness is my supply; my consciousness is my health; my consciousness is my good." Why? Because God has planted in us His son, whose mission it is to heal the sick, raise the dead, feed the hungry. This Son, this Christ, is embodied in every individual. "I have meat to eat that ye know not of."[6] I have this hidden Christ, this "hidden manna."[7]

Building the New Consciousness by Abiding in the Word

If we abide in this truth, we will bear fruit richly, but if not, we will be as a branch of a tree that is cut off, withers, and dies. Who, then, is going to ensure our progress on the Way? Who but we ourselves? And how? By whether we abide in the Word of whether we are determined to live by bread alone, whether we decide that our amusements are going to be all of the external variety. This does not mean that we should not enjoy music, the theater, art, literature, or other harmless forms of pleasure that come to us. It only means not to live by these exclusively. We must live by the Word, and the Word is the indwelling Christ, the indwelling spirit of God. We must place our reliance there and not outside in a bank account or in our family, not outside on external pleasures. It means reserving some period of every day for the realization:

> The kingdom of God is within me.
> The Son of God, the Christ dwelleth in me,
> and Its function is to manifest
> as harmony and peace
> in every avenue of my experience.

We may have some problems even when we are living in the Word. We have not yet reached such a high degree of Christ-consciousness that we avoid all the mesmerism of human sense; but at least we have a remedy, at least we have an antidote, something to which we can have recourse.

We are building our Christ-consciousness as we abide in the spiritual Word, but we are also building it when we become a part of the "two or three. . . gathered together in my name,"[8] in the very name and nature of this spiritual word. In such a gathering, someone may have gone one step higher than others, and those who are that one step higher lift the others into the higher consciousness. We never know who in that state of heightened awareness is lifting us to his level. The advantage of coming together as one of the two or more gathered in this spiritual name is that we can be assured that we are developing the new man in us. In proportion as we are, the old man is dying.

If, when a person is no longer studying this letter, some of these words come back to his consciousness and he allows them to have a place in his consciousness, he is adding to the work that has already been done, and in that degree the new man is increasing in him, and the old man is decreasing. Then when tomorrow comes along, he must continue to abide in truth.

To What Extent Are We Rejecting Appearances?

To what extent do we permit spiritual truth to occupy our consciousness beyond the reading we do? Here I must inject a word of caution. It is not the reading, in and of itself, that will develop our consciousness, but what we do with what we read. We might read a whole chapter of an inspiring book, but if we pass by some form of sin, disease, or false appetite out on the street, or wherever we may witness it, without ministering to it, we are losing the opportunity of developing the new man in us and letting the old one die.

If we accept appearances, the old man is still living in us; but if, when we see sin, disease, lack, or accident, we let these words of truth live in us and then say, "I must not accept appearances: I must accept God as omnipresence," not only may we heal, uplift, reform, or forgive someone, but some part of the old man of us has died in the moment that we applied a truth to a specific situation. That truth came alive in us, but it could come only out of the new man. It cannot come out of the old man, because there is no truth in the old man, no truth in him at all. He "is not subject to the law of God, neither indeed can be."[9]

We all know the little annoyances of family life. The very closeness of living with two, three, or four human beings breeds irritations. The old man lives in constant complaint about it, allowing himself to be influenced by the outer conditions, responding to them with fault-finding and exasperation. But in proportion as a word of truth can come into our consciousness and we say, "Ah, no, that is that little old man popping up again. Ah, no! There is an indwelling Christ in me, in him, in her," in that degree we have shown forth the new man that is developing in us. In proportion, then, as we no longer react to appearances, as they humanly are, in that degree can we tell how rapidly we are dying to the old man, and being reborn to the new.

Are We Mesmerized
by the News?

The newspapers, radio, and television give us the news of the day, and it is possible to determine the degree of our progress on the path by our reaction to that news. If we fear all the bad news, the old man is very much in charge of us. If we have come to the point of saying, "Yes, that is the human scene, the carnal mind, but fortunately I know that my life is dependent on God, that all life, real life, is dependent on God, not on man. Fortunately, I know that in the last analysis, nobody is going to find a system for making all of us prosperous; therefore, I do not have to fear what these men are doing. My individual prosperity is going to be the showing forth of my own state of consciousness.

There have been men who have become millionaires in panic times, and there have been millionaires who have lost everything they had in boom times. The times do not make a person wealthy or poor: it is what is taking place in his consciousness that makes him wealthy or poor. So, if we are fearing the Common Market or if we are fearing a new administration, we are reacting; the old man is working in us. But if we can hear or read all this news and realize, "My fate is not dependent on 'man, whose breath is in his nostrils.'[10] My fate is dependent on the degree of God-consciousness I attain," the new man has been born in us, and is being developed.

By these signs we can see that we really are passing from the stage of the old man to the stage of the new man, from the stage of the natural man who is not under the law of God to the stage of that man who has his being in Christ and who is under the law of God. We are passing from the human state of consciousness to the spiritual in proportion to the effort, the time, and the devotion that we give to our spiritual studies, meditations, and practice.

Losing Concepts of God

When we are helpless children, our parents and our churches present concepts of God to us which we have no way of denying or refuting, and because of the authority vested in our parents and institutions, these concepts can easily be forced upon us. Few there are who are able to overcome their early conditioning to the extent of discarding the concepts of God to which they were introduced in childhood. Few there are who can themselves begin to seek and search for God. One generation passes on its concept of God and truth to the next. Then comes the struggle to overcome those early concepts when a person discovers that the God he has been worshiping is not doing for him what the true God would be doing if he knew that God and could make contact with It.

Mankind has failed to find God and has been worshiping idols, mental images in thought of one form or another. Here and there, throughout the ages, there are men who have discovered the one and only God, and each of these has revealed this God to his followers, disciples, apostles, and students. Nearly always, however, the vision of the true God has been lost.

The Master gave his life that it might be revealed that God is in the midst of us, that His name is *I,* so that never again would we look up to heaven for God, look for God in holy mountains, in holy temples, or in holy books, but that we would realize that the place whereon we stand is holy ground because *I Am* there.

I, the mighty one, am in the midst of you,
and *I* will never leave you nor forsake you.

Do you hunger? Take no thought for baker's bread
or butcher's meat, for you have in the midst
of you the *I* that *I Am,*

and *I* am your meat, and your bread,
and your wine, and your water.

If you will look unto this *I* in the midst of you,
I will set a table before you in the wilderness.
I will set a table before you in the wilderness—
nobody else: not friends, not relatives, not bankers.
I will set a table before you in the wilderness if you
will look unto the *I* that *I Am* in the midst of you.

Once we have received this revelation, we are free. We are living and moving and having our being in God, and God in us.

Is it any wonder that many men have been persecuted unto death for revealing to the people that which will give them their eternal freedom, so that once knowing this they never again will be in bondage to any man or system of men? There is no might and there is no power that can withstand the knowledge of God. "Come unto me, all ye that labor and are heavy laden, and I will give you rest."[11] When we come unto this *I* that is within us, no shackles will ever be placed on our Soul, on our mind, or on our body. But this is only as we learn to know God aright.

Lose the Old Man by Recognizing I

Just as there have been the many worlds and the many gods, so you and I individually have been many persons; but in spite of the many masks we have worn, we are still two persons, and one of these must die. One of us must be put off, and that one is our mortal selfhood, that selfhood which is a sense of separation from God. That cannot be lifted up and made spiritual. One of the mistakes of the ages has been the belief that we can take the "natural man,"[12] the human being, and make him spiritual and turn him into the son of God. This we cannot do. The "creature,"[13] that which Paul called the natural man, must be put off. The man of earth must be put off; mortality must be taken from us and immortality revealed.

To accomplish this death of mortal man, so that we may be reborn of the Spirit, that we may be raised up into the stature of manhood in Christ Jesus, we must recognize *I* at the center of our being and realize Its name, Its nature, and Its function. Why does the Master say, "I am come that they might have life, and that they might have it more abundantly"[14]? We must individually acknowledge that there has been this I who was born, that is doomed to die, this I that at times has been a pretty good man or woman and other times not, this selfhood which is mortality itself that has existed and to some extent still exists, and that we are in the process of dying daily. But we must also acknowledge there is an *I* within us at the center of our being that has come that we might have life eternal.

I am with you. *I* have always been with you awaiting
your recognition. *I* will never leave you.
Rest in Me. Put your faith, your hope, and your
confidence in the truth that *I* am in the midst of you,
and that *I* am God. Be still and know that *I* in the
midst of you am God, and that *I* will never leave you,
that *I* am your bread, your meat, and your water.
Cease from dependence on man, whose breath
is in his nostrils. Know that *I* live in you
and you live in Me, for we are one,
and really *I* am you. *I* am the Word that becomes
flesh as you. *I* am the Word by which you live.

I am your comforter: *I* am your healer.
I am come that you might be made whole—
not for threescore years and ten, but forever,
for *I* am your eternal life, *I* am your eternal being.
I am your spiritual, immortal being.

Such meditation reveals that we are not this man of earth as we have thought ourselves to be; we are not this human being born of woman, living for a few days only. We are the offspring of God, the infinite, the divine Creator of all that is, and that God found everything that He created to be good.

Truths Stored in Consciousness Bring the Reaping

One touch of the Spirit in meditation can lift us over a thousand-year period, and a thousand years can be encompassed in a second. If that meditation touches us in the right way, in one moment we can die as Saul of Tarsus did and be reborn in the next minute as Paul. Many have had that experience. Many have had the experience of dying in a moment, but we can be assured that those who died in a moment had much preparation before it in seeking truth.

The point is, however, that every bit of preparation, every bit of scriptural study, every bit of metaphysical practice in which we are denying the reality of power in the external and affirming the all-power of our consciousness is leading us to a moment when we can jump forward a thousand years in spiritual development. Until such time, we have no real way of knowing what progress we are making. These truths are being embodied in our consciousness; they are being stored up; and until something brings them forth, we may not even realize that they are there.

This reminds me of the man who came to me from a certain church in my first year of practice. He was badly crippled with arthritis, and in a period of a few months he had a beautiful healing. There was a woman in the same church who was also crippled with arthritis and wanted very much to be healed. She was one of these dear old church-type ladies. They brought her to my office, and I began to talk to her about her spiritual identity, assuring her that she was the child of God. She nearly took my head off. "I am a poor worm of the dust. I am not fit to touch the hem of His robe. Do not talk to me that way! This is a sin!"

"Well," I said, "I must tell you the truth."

"That is not the truth! I know what I am!"

This was my first year of practice, and I can assure you that I was eager to seize every opportunity for healing work. So I said, "I will tell you what we will do. We will not talk truth any more: we will just have silent prayer." That was good, because she would not have to hear any more of that.

She was brought to my office one day every week, and I never spoke to her of truth again; we would just have our silent treatment. One day in the midst of the winter, as she was leaving the building and going through a revolving door, her foot touched a piece of ice and she went right through and on out into the middle of the road. The doorman, sensing a lawsuit, ran out to pick her up, and she said, "Do not touch me; do not touch me! I am the child of God!" She telephoned me the next day that her arthritis was all gone and she was feeling fine, but she felt that she had committed such a sin in making that remark that she never would come back again.

Once an idea touches our consciousness, we may not know it is there, but some emergency arises, and out of it comes this that has been latent within us. With all our reading, truth is lodging itself in our consciousness, and this is transforming us. We are being renewed inwardly, day by day, with every bit of truth that we take into our consciousness. It is growing in there in a cumulative way, and gradually the time comes when we can look back and see parts of ourselves that are now dead.

Measuring Progress

Sometimes as I look back, I can see myself sitting in a room playing cards, smoking cigars, and drinking highballs, and I think, "That could not have been me. That must have been two other people." And it could not have been me, because I could not any more do it now than I could jump off the roof. That is a memory that I am retaining of somebody I once knew, and fortunately he is dead and buried, and I have nothing left but a memory.

Now, there are other parts of me, too, that I can look back on and see that they are dead: fears and doubts. When a person is living out from human consciousness, everything in this world is to be feared. But that man is gone. So with us. Unless we can look back five years, seven years, ten years, we cannot possibly know the parts of us that have died.

One student who was very close to her ninetieth birthday traveled thousands of miles to come to our 1962 class in Hawaii. Talking with her one day, she said, "You know, what embarrasses me is the people who come to me and say that I am so wonderful for my age. But I am not any different from what I was forty years ago!" And of course she was not. She had no consciousness of time, no consciousness of age, and so it did not seem to her to be a miracle. To others who expect a person at ninety to be half-way buried, it is a miracle.

The call upon us is to forsake that false identity, that natural man, that creature, that man whose breath is in his nostrils, to let him die as we are reborn by acknowledging:

I in the midst of me is God, and that *I* has created
me in Its own image and likeness. All the infinite,
divine life of God is the life of my individual being.
I have access to the *I* that is within me, which is
God, for I and the Father are one. I am the expression, the manifestation, the offspring of the infinite,
divine *I* that I am, and this *I* is forever in the midst
of me that I might have life, and that
I might have it more abundantly.

In quietness and in confidence truth will be revealed to us from the center of our being. Where else can we go for truth, if the kingdom of God is within us? We do not need to accept the word of a man, a woman, or of a book. We have the divine right to go to the center of our own being and ask the question:

Father, who am I? Father, what am I?
Father, for what purpose was I created in Thy image
and likeness? I know that as a human being I am not
fulfilling any divine function. I know that as a
human being my days are numbered. I have missed
the way. Now reveal Thyself and Thy plan,
and Thy name, and Thy nature, and my relationship
to Thee, and Thy relationship to me.

If we are sincere truth-seekers, eventually all truth must be revealed to us from within, for every man must be taught of God. No teacher is worthy the name of teacher who does not reveal to us that we have access to the entire kingdom of God, of Truth, of Life within ourselves, and that we are dependent on no man, no teacher, no teaching. We are dependent only on *I* who sent us into expression.

Those who have been the great revelators of truth throughout all ages have survived in the heart, soul, and consciousness of mankind because each one turned us to the kingdom within ourselves, showing us the full and complete nature of our identity, of our relationship to Infinity.

There is a dying process, but it is not the death of the body or the death of the mind or soul. It is inwardly refusing to accept anything about ourselves that is not of a spiritual nature. At first it is difficult. It is hard to put off that old man who likes some people and dislikes others, who likes some nations or races and does not like others. It is a difficult process until we dig down and find that because there is only one Father underneath we are brothers and sisters. The thing that has set up a sense of separation is the lies we have been told about each other.

Our Destiny and Divine Purpose

We must put off that old man who believed that he was born on a certain day and has just a certain number of years to live, changing, altering, and weakening as the years go by. Instead must come the realization:

> I am life eternal. I am immortal.
> I am the offspring of the spiritual, most high,
> infinite, divine Being, and the life that is God is the
> life that is mine, for these are one. My life is eternal,
> immortal, unaging, undying, unchanging.

In this way we are dying to that old man, who has infirmities, and we are being reborn to the man we really are, the being we really are: immortal being, divine being, spiritual being. With this comes the first faint glimpse of why we were born, why we are on earth, and why God sent us forth into expression. We stop thinking of our mother and father as our parents and think of them only as instruments through which we came to earth, and go behind and beyond them with this question: "Who sent me? What sent me? And why?"

Even while we acknowledge our parents as the instruments through which God sent us to earth, we know it was God that sent us to earth. Our parents were but the instruments: they were caretakers for us. They were given the responsibility of our mind and body and soul to care for until we were out of those two years in Egypt and strong enough to stand on our own feet. It was God who sent us forth to earth, God who sent us forth into being, and for God's purpose, for a spiritual purpose and a divine purpose.

What is that purpose? Scripture tells us clearly that we were sent here to show forth God's glory, just as the heavens declare the glory of God, and the earth shows forth His handiwork. So do we, the greatest creation of God, glorify God by being alive, not in our humanhood, however, for heaven knows we are nothing that God can be proud of in our humanhood. But there is an *I* of us, there is a being, there is a spiritual identity which has for its purpose showing forth God's glory: not testifying to our greatness, to our wisdom, to our love, to our benevolence, but testifying only to God expressing through us, God revealing Himself on earth through us that we may be brothers and sisters, that we may enjoy life and bring forth some spiritual function on earth, just as there is a spiritual function in heaven.

We have no way of knowing what our progress is. There is only one thing that we can measure, and that is our integrity. We can measure that. We know right well whether we are cheating on the time, effort, and devotion we give to our spiritual studies. We know whether we are spending too much time in a direction in which we have no right to be going while we should be at our spiritual studies, meditations, and practice. Of course, every time we face ourselves in that way, we might as well acknowledge this: As I am sowing, so am I reaping. That to which I give my consciousness in this minute is determining that which is coming forth from my consciousness next week, next month, next year, or ten years from now. So if I really want to die to the old man, even if at the moment there seems to be no fruitage from it, "I press toward the mark for the prize of the high calling of God in Christ Jesus."[15]

ACROSS THE DESK

During this month of May, rise into the consciousness of this letter by studying diligently its lesson, a message to help your progress on the capital path, so that you may be that "new man" with the life-giving experience of rebirth.

But the mere study of this letter is not enough. With it must come the day by day and moment by moment practice of transferring power from the realm of effect to the kingdom within where all power is to be found. It takes alertness, but is that not worthwhile in the light of the goal? Is any effort too great to obtain that?

Chapter Six

Building the Transcendental Consciousness

Illumination, the attainment of spiritual consciousness or that mind that was also in Christ Jesus, comes when there has been sufficient inner preparation. That preparation consists not only of regular meditation and of learning the letter of truth, but what is even more essential: the practice of it. The letter of truth itself does not do the work of producing harmony in our experience: it merely helps to bring about a change of consciousness.

Living Out from the Principle of One Power

Let me illustrate that. In our ordinary human state we are always fearing the power of evil in one way or another, fearing infection, contagion, age, lack, fearing tyrants, domination or those who dominate, or fearing the weather, storms, lightning, wild animals, beasts, and reptiles.

In this divided state of consciousness where we have respect for the power of good and yet fear the power of evil, there is very little possibility of attaining illumination. But when we accept the spiritual principle that there is but one real Power and therefore we need not fear any negative or evil powers, we begin an

actual practice of that way of living and whenever we are con-
fronted with an erroneous appearance we consciously remember:

There is but one power.
I need not fear what man can do to me;
I need not fear what mortal conditions can do to me;
I need not fear what germs or animals can do to me;
I need not fear what bullets or bombs can do to me
because all power is spiritual power.
There is but one power.

We abide in that word of truth and let it abide in us, and
gradually we begin to lose our fear of external forces and powers and come to a state of consciousness where even though we
see or hear about them yet we know no fear of them. In the
degree that we do not react to anything with fear or concern, we
have attained some measure of illumination. That illumination
is in proportion to our lack of fear of anything external. Since
the kingdom of God is within us, since the realm of power and
dominion is within us, there is nothing external that can bring
harm, be destructive or injurious to us.

In the human state of consciousness, where it is normal and
natural to believe in two powers, this is not true. There are
many things external to us that are harmful. In fact, there are
more things in the external world that are harmful than are
good. It is only as our consciousness changes that we perceive
the truth that the power is within.

All power flows out from me
since the kingdom of God is within me.
No power flows to me: all power is within me.
Since I and the Father are one,
I am infinite; and therefore there are
no powers external to me.

As we abide in that truth and let that truth abide in us, gradually we lose the fear that certain foods do not agree with us or that certain weather affects us. But now these things do not disturb us. In other words, as our individual consciousness on the subject of power changes, so does this world change in its effect upon us, and while a thousand may fall at our left and ten thousand at our right, it will not come nigh the dwelling place of those who have accepted the principle of one Power and are practicing it and living in it until it becomes a definite settled state of consciousness.

Recognizing God As Individual Being

Human beings like some people and dislike other people; they trust some and distrust or fear others; they love some and hate others. All this is because their consciousness has not been illumined on the subject of impersonalization.

God constitutes individual being. God is the life, the mind, the soul, and the Spirit of every individual. When that truth is accepted and realized, all individuals become instruments of God's goodness, and every individual is an avenue or a channel for God's grace.

If we look out from our human eyes, we will not believe this and will not see it, but if we can at first accept the revelation of those who have been spiritually illumined throughout the ages, we will discover that it has been revealed that God constitutes individual man, woman, child, and animal. Therefore, we are all one in spiritual brotherhood.

Once we perceive this, we are able to impersonalize evil because we know that the traits of character of Mr. Jones, Mr. Brown, and Mr. Smith are not their traits. They are the universal belief in two powers, the carnal mind: they are impersonal. Thus we separate them from the individual who seems to be an avenue or outlet for them. In doing this, we not only make ourselves immune to the suggestions of the carnal mind but very often heal the other person.

The Realization of Spiritual Identity, a Protective Influence

Many of you may have heard the story of the banker who had been so trained to understand the spiritual nature of man that it had become part of his very mind and soul to realize this truth in every situation. Every Friday night, this man was in the habit of carrying home a payroll to deliver to a factory on Saturday morning. One night he left the bank with his brief case filled with money, and on approaching a piece of property that he had to cross, something came to him that seemed to say he had forgotten something at the bank. He turned around and went back although he could not for the moment remember what he had forgotten. He felt, however, that he had forgotten something, but when he went inside the bank, he discovered he had forgotten nothing. He could not understand why he had returned there because, after searching around, there was not a single thing he had forgotten or left undone. So he locked the bank and started back for his home, arriving there safely.

The next morning, he read in the newspaper that in that very street at the particular piece of property that he was about to cross there had been a holdup, which occurred within a few minutes of the time that he had turned back to the bank to find what he thought he had forgotten. He tried to think whether it had any connection with what had happened to him the night before, and when the two men who had committed this holdup were caught, he asked permission to see them. He asked them if they knew him, and one of them said, "Oh, yes, you are the banker; you are the man we were after. But when you first came to the street and turned around and went back, we could not get to you. When you came back the second time, you had those other two men with you, and we were not going to tackle three of you."

Who were the other two men with him? Since there was no other person with him, obviously it was the divine protective influence that had come forth from his own inner consciousness, a protective influence that came because of his continuous dwelling in the realization that God constitutes individual being. With that as a conviction, no evil could come nigh his dwelling place. There would always be a protective influence about him even if, as on that occasion, it had to externalize itself and appear as two men. As a matter of fact, there were not two men: there was just this spiritual protective influence which his own state of consciousness had created.

If we live consciously in the realization that God constitutes individual being, that God is the life and the mind and the soul of every individual, that purity of consciousness will be a protective influence, and it will prevent evil coming near us because evil never comes to the pure in thought.

The pure in thought are not the ignorant, who have no awareness of life. The pure in thought are those who understand the purity of man's spiritual nature. As we entertain this in consciousness, practice and live with it, regardless of whom we see or what his nature or character may be, as we dwell constantly in the realization of God as constituting individual being, we develop for ourselves an illumined consciousness that will not permit evil to touch us and will throw around us a protective atmosphere. There again, the correct letter of truth, when known and practiced, transforms consciousness and develops a higher state of consciousness.

Applying Spiritual Promises to Daily Experience

Every spiritual principle we learn has an effect on our consciousness and plays its part in transforming it. In our human experience, we are always meeting problems that are a little bit too much for us, a little too difficult to solve, or problems that we fear we might not be able to solve. When we enter this spiritual path, we read in scripture such passages as these: "Thou wilt keep him in perfect peace, whose mind is stayed on thee.[1] . . . Trust in the Lord with all thine heart; and lean not unto thine own understanding. In all thy ways acknowledge him, and he shall direct thy paths.[2]. . . He performeth the thing that is appointed for me.[3] . . . The Lord will perfect that which concerneth me.[4]. . . Greater is he that is in you, than he that is in the world."[5]

If we read such passages often enough, memorize some of them, and then each day apply them as a difficult problem arises, one which we think we may not be able to solve of ourselves and we remember, "Ah, yes, But I alone do not have to solve it. There is a He that is within me, and He is greater than he that is within the world. There is a He that performeth that which is given me to do. There is a Presence that goes before me to make the way straight; there is a Presence that goes to prepare mansions for me," we are being transformed in consciousness to where a problem out here is no longer a problem of ours alone but a problem of ours and the Father's.

A Divine Partnership

Now we are building a consciousness where we are no longer just individuals living our own life, fighting our battles, having to do everything for ourselves. Now we have a partnership: "I and my Father are one.[6]. . . I can of mine own self do nothing.[7]. . . The Father that dwelleth in me, he doeth the works.[8]. . . I will go before thee, and make the crooked places straight."[9]

Is it not clear how, by doing this, we are developing a whole new consciousness where there is no longer just we by ourselves. There is "I and my Father." Between the two of us we can lick the world. In fact, I suspect He can do it without me, but then it is good to know that He and I are partners.

If we have a Bible and merely read all those statements, it may do nothing for us; if we simply quote those statements, they may do nothing for us; but if we work with them, apply them each day with every problem that comes up, it would not be many months before we would have such an awareness of this Presence that never again would we feel that we had an unsurmountable problem or even a very difficult one because, regardless of how difficult the problem, it is not really we who have to solve it. There is always a He. There is an invisible Presence, an infinite Presence that not only is where we are, since the kingdom is within us, but because of the nature of It as omnipresent, It also goes before us adjusting everything that needs adjusting and supplying everything that needs supplying.

Once we attain the consciousness of that transcendental Presence, which in Christian mysticism is called the Christ, in the Hebrew the Messiah, and which in the Orient has many names, eventually we build within ourselves an absolute assurance that we are never alone. Every day brings evidence of what happens to us when we have an evolved consciousness of a divine Presence. If, as like that banker, we walk out into danger, we will find that the consciousness of that Presence may appear as two armed guards beside us or two policemen; or if we were in the water, even if we could not swim, we would find ourselves safe at the shore.

A couple of years ago a student was overturned in a boat two miles from shore in a storm; the sails and paddles were lost; and yet he reached shore safely and for one reason only: a continuous recognition of the Presence. There was no way for him to reach that shore, no human way, but there was a consciousness of the Presence, the awareness of "I will never leave thee, nor forsake thee,"[10] and so just by paddling with his hands in the water he finally made it.

When we have that consciousness of the Presence, we do

not have to take thought for every single detail of our life; we do not have to plan it all out to the last dot. There is always Something greater than we are, helping us in our endeavors, but it is we who develop that consciousness, and we develop it by the practice of these principles. By applying the principle of one Power, we develop the consciousness of the nonpower of anything in the external world. By practicing the Presence of this He that is within us, we develop a consciousness of the Presence, and then there is always Something greater than our human capacity functioning for us and within us.

Losing Fear of Material Law

Many persons fear material or physical laws and, sometimes as metaphysicians, they even fear mental laws. But there is no reason for this because if we faithfully practice the principle of one law, of God as the law-giver, we will so abide in the realization that all law is spiritual, therefore perfect and harmonious, that never will we find occasion to fear a material law, not even the law of the calendar. But it is we who must know the truth; it is we who must practice the correct letter of truth so that we develop this consciousness.

Losing Fear of and for People

To the world of appearances, our greatest fears are man and man's potentiality for doing evil. We fear those who have taken the wrong path in life. We fear those who have entered the arena of politics with wrong motives. We fear for our children when they are growing up because we think they may be led astray into doing evil things. All this, however is dissipated as we acquire the consciousness of God as individual being.

Regardless of the fact that children seem to be very human, very mischievous, very everything that children can be, every parent should carry inside himself the realization of God as constituting their soul, mind, and Spirit, consciously remembering that even their body is the temple of the living God. This helps to keep their bodies pure. Thus the parent builds such a consciousness within himself of God's life, God's law, and God's spirit as constituting the individual that all those who are within range of his consciousness come under that Grace instead of under the law.

The Old Man Lives Under the Law

This illumined consciousness that we are seeking, and in part attaining, will ultimately bring out the experience that the Master tried to give us in leading us out of life under the Hebraic law into the new life that is to be lived by Grace. We must understand first of all that the Master recognized two states of consciousness. His statement, "My kingdom is not of this world,"[11] indicated clearly that as far as he was concerned there were two states of consciousness. The nature of those states of consciousness is revealed by John: "For the law was given by Moses, but grace and truth came by Jesus Christ."[12] It is important that we understand clearly the meaning of this, because this also is part of the goal that we are attempting to attain on the spiritual path, and in a measure are attaining.

As human beings, we live entirely under the law. We are governed by physical and mental laws, but the greatest law of all, and the one that has really worked havoc in the life of mankind, is the law of as-ye-sow-so-shall-ye-reap, that which has been called karma or karmic law. Actually karmic law is the same as the law of as-ye-sow-so-shall-ye-reap: as we do to another so will it be done unto us. As human beings, we have been living under that law. Every time we have thought, yes, even thought, anything unkind about anyone, untrue, malicious, or sensual, we have set in motion the law of karma, the law of as-ye-sow-so-shall-ye-reap. We have decreed for ourselves what we have just sent out. We are calling back unto ourselves that which we have just done to or thought about another. Without question, it is certainly coming back to us.

As a matter of fact, the Master said that we do not necessarily have to kill a man in order to have punishment come back to us. "Whosoever is angry with his brother without a cause shall be in danger of the judgment.[13]. . . Whosoever looketh on a woman to lust after her hath committed adultery with her already in his heart."[14] Just to think of it! That is very strong medicine when we stop to think how uncontrolled our thoughts have been at times with anger, with resentment, with something of an unjust nature, something of an untrue nature, gossip or scandal. Then we sometimes wonder why this has come upon us or that, and we feel we did not deserve it. Now we know we did; now we know that we set in motion the very evil that has come upon us.

That is the way we live as human beings, but the Master was trying to lift us into another consciousness where this law does not operate, where there is no longer a law of weather to affect us, a law of matter, a law of poison, a law of germs, or a law of karma. His entire mission was to lift us into a state of life where the law does not operate, where karma does not operate. Christians have missed the point entirely, and so these last seventeen hundred years the Christian world has been living under the law instead of under Grace.

Coming Under Grace

What is Grace? Grave is living in absolute, complete harmony in every department of our life, living without might, without power, without effort, without taking thought, without earning our livelihood by human conniving or without being deserving of it. Life comes to us as a gift of God, as heirs of God. Think of that and consider carefully this passage from Romans:

> For to be carnally minded is death;
> but to be spiritually minded is life and peace.
> Because the carnal mind is enmity against God: for it
> is not subject to the law of God,
> neither indeed can be.
> So then they that are in the flesh cannot please God.
> But ye are not in the flesh, but in the Spirit,
> if so be the Spirit of God dwell in you.
>
> Romans 8:6-9

As human beings we are not under the law of God, not under the grace of God, not receiving the gift of God, the protection of God, or the support of God, but "if so be the spirit of God dwell in you," all this is wiped out, and then we live by being heirs. We do not struggle for anything: we inherit everything. We do not strive: we receive it as a gift of God, as the grace of God. This is what the Master taught, and the world has been too blind to accept it. How do we come out from under the law and have the spirit of God dwelling in us so that we become children of God and live by Grace? The first step is to review the Sermon on the Mount and see what the Master taught must be given up, in other words, review that part which deals with the ye-have-heard-it-said-of-old and then that part where he says, "But I say unto you."[15] We have to become consciously aware that we are trying to fulfill that side of the Sermon on the Mount.

Rising Above Sowing and Reaping

It can be simplified by realizing every day and, if necessary, several times a day:

> I of my own self can do nothing either evil or good.
> I of my own self wish to do neither evil nor good.

> I wish only to be an instrument
> through which God's love reaches the world—
> not my love, God's love; not my gifts, God's gifts;
> not my goodness, God's goodness.

Each day let us be sure to realize that whatever of a negative nature is still in our consciousness is not ours: it is impersonal; it is of the carnal mind; and therefore, it can produce no evil, and also realize that whatever of good is in our consciousness is not our good: it is God's good.

When we do this, we are dying daily to ourselves, we are coming out from under the law, because now we are not sowing evil and we are not sowing good. Therefore, we will not reap evil and we will not reap good. Now we will neither sow nor reap: we will be the instruments of God's grace. As long as there is a sowing and a reaping, there is an "I" doing it, but the moment we are no longer sowing or reaping there is only God shining through.

If we say to ourselves, "I will withhold evil," we are giving ourselves too much credit, as if we were giving ourselves credit for being good because we want to withhold evil. This, we must not do. We must realize that evil is not a power; evil has no person in whom, on whom, or through whom to operate: it is a nothingness. And what about good? No, there is no good in you or in me to be done. "Why callest thou me good? there is none good but one, that is, God."[16]

> Let me be used only by the Father;
> let God's good and God's grace
> flow through me to everyone I meet:
> friend or foe, white or black,
> Jew or Gentile, Protestant or Catholic.
> Let me be an instrument through which God's grace
> flows to the saint and the sinner alike.

Ascribe No Qualities to a Person

The Master never held anyone in judgment except those supposed to be in high spiritual places; those he called bad names. When we see someone wearing the robe of virtue and righteousness in high places and being cancerous underneath, it is probably all right to take the horsewhip to them and drive them out of the temple, but not otherwise, because those in high places who are consciously doing evil sometimes need a rough awakening. But on the whole, it is safe for us to adopt the principle of no judgment, no criticism, no condemnation, and the willingness that God's grace flow to anyone and everyone within range of our consciousness, near or far, saint or sinner.

We come out from under the law and come under Grace when we no longer ascribe evil to ourselves or to another, but always impersonalize it; and above all, when we do not ascribe qualities of good to ourselves. Let us never fool ourselves by believing that we are good, that we are philanthropic, that we are charitable, that we are gentle, because we of ourselves are none of those things. If such qualities are finding expression through us, it is because God is finding expression through us, and all of those qualities belong to God. If temporarily any bit of evil should find outlet through us, let us not condemn ourselves, but immediately impersonalize it and realize that this too is not of us: it is the carnal mind which temporarily we have let find expression. In our recognition of that, it is as if we were repenting.

Impersonalization Leads to the Higher Consciousness

Repentance is the word the Master gave us; repentance is the essential thing; and repentance does not mean wearing sackcloth and ashes or standing up against the wailing wall and crying about our past misdeeds. Repentance means the acknowledgment that we have been guilty, coupled with the declaration that we do not mean to let it happen again insofar as it lies within our power.

We impersonalize the evil so that we do not condemn ourselves or another, but we also impersonalize good so that we recognize that whatever good is flowing through us or another is really God finding outlet and expression. In this way, we pass from living under the law to living under Grace.

We are under Grace in proportion as there is no longer a personal I within us to do evil or to do good. We are taught to die daily, and dying daily does not mean changing bad into good. It means letting the personal sense of I disappear as rapidly as we can so that we live in the consciousness of whatever evil there is as impersonal and a nothingness. Whatever good there is, is the grace of God. That leaves the little I out of the picture. What freedom it gives us if we are engaged in a profession or a business and realize that we are not dependent on the human mind, but that there is a Christ-mind within us ready to perform for us the moment we are still!

If we continue going through life as if we were doing it wholly on our own, we could not fail to recognize the difficulties we would face and sometimes the impossibility of meeting them. There are times when our problems will not dissolve. But it is then that we must have a complete or a clear recognition that there is a Father within us, and that It has a function. There is a kingdom of God within us, and It has a function. There is the spirit of the Lord upon us, and It has a function.

When we enter into a consciousness of life that acknowledges our partnership with the Father and that even though we are one, the Father is greater than we are, and the Father goes before us, we are developing the transcendental consciousness which is called the Christ. When we develop that consciousness, we will find that the things of this world do not come near our dwelling place, at least not to the extent they formerly did.

A young boy of twelve wrote me a letter sometime ago telling me that his work in school was good except in the subject of mathematics. On a particular day he faced an examination and when he looked at the questions, he knew he was lost because he had no answers. The whole thing seemed strange and impossible to him. He had been studying the pamphlet, "Lesson to Sam," and in the midst of the examination, the thought came to him, "There is a mind within me that knows all things; there is this Spirit within me." For a moment, he became very still, and then when he opened his eyes, he saw the whole thing and the answers, and he not only wrote a good examination, but from that time on, his school work improved.

What is the answer to that? It is a consciousness of the presence of a transcendental Something that is a higher mind than our human mind, a higher wisdom than man's wisdom. "Lean not unto thine own understanding." Would it not be wonderful if every child carried that into school! Would it not be wonderful if everyone who had a business or a profession carried that one statement with him and sat and meditated a moment to let the divine Wisdom reveal Itself to him, to let this inner Wisdom come forth!

By using the correct letter of truth as found in scripture and spiritual writings with which to build this higher consciousness, then when the higher consciousness is upon us, we no longer need the letter of truth except for the purpose of teaching.

The letter of truth as given in all the writings is the tool. It is given to use and practice so that we may develop a consciousness entirely different from the one with which we were born. Through the study and practice of the principles, a consciousness is developed that no longer fears or hates anything because of the recognition of one Power. A consciousness is developed which is a complete recognition of God as constituting individual being. A consciousness of the partnership of "I and my Father" is gradually attained.

ACROSS THE DESK

Often when we sit down to meditate, our mind seems to be churning with thoughts about people, conditions, and ideas that appear as problems to be solved. This is, of course, the result of the universal belief or universal hypnotism that claims that there are two powers. Instead of letting the mind keep going around and around over these problems, we turn from them, knowing that we have the capacity to govern the mind because it is our instrument:

> My mind is not a battleground for the belief in two
> powers: my mind is an avenue through which the I of
> my being flows. As the pure unconditioned mind, it
> is untouched by carnal thought and is an open door
> for the outpouring of the beauty and truth of God's
> kingdom from the eternal Source within my being.

Since this is a universal truth, it is the truth about every individual.

After such a realization, it is easier to settle down, relax, and listen until the release comes from within. The constant pressures of this world bring moments to all of us when it seems that there is more than one Power, and at such times we must be alert to this temptation. Instead of capitulating to the temptation, we take possession of our mind and put it in its proper place as our instrument, subject to our direction, our servant rather than our master. The following two chapters from the writings should help you do this:

"Dominion Over Mind, Body, and Purse,"
Our Spiritual Resources

"Unconditioned Mind," *The Thunder of Silence*

TAPE RECORDED EXCERPTS
Prepared by the Editor

Life, in which we rely entirely on our own strength and wisdom, can be sometimes good and sometimes bad. But when we draw on the infinite treasures of that Something within greater than ourselves, less and less are we victims of circumstances and more and more do we come into conscious dominion, watching life unfold joyously from day to day, knowing that the responsibility is no longer ours but rests on His shoulders.

Joel emphasized the importance of constantly practicing the Presence and thus being consciously aware of Its activity in our experience. The following excerpts show different ways in which we can acknowledge Him.

Practicing the Presence

"I can of my own self do nothing. It is the Father within me that does the work, and I am in the Father, and the Father is in me. The entire air that surrounds me is an ocean of God, and it fills me outside and inside. I live and move and have my being in this ocean of God, in this sea of Love and Wisdom. I am in God, and God is in me. I dwell in the secret place of the most High. . . . I live in God. . . .

"I soar up into the atmosphere, still surrounded by the everlasting life and the everlasting love which is the nature of God. I cannot escape from His arms. Underneath are the everlasting arms. I live and move and have my being in Him. I rest in Him. . . .

"I live, not by might or by power, but by God's grace. I can rest in the assurance of God's grace. . . . If at the moment I appear to be barren of health or wealth or opportunity, I realize that the presence of God in me is the assurance that in due season I, too, will bear fruit richly. . . ."

Joel S. Goldsmith, "The Ten Second Meditations,"
The 1962 Princess Kaiulani Open Class.

"God is the only power. Nothing, not even drunken drivers
on the road, can have power. Only God can have power. Not
even my mistakes can have power. Only God can have power. .
. . I have all the power of God with me in every transaction, in
every experience, in every journey. Every step of my way, I have
Omnipresence, Omnipotence. . . ."

Joel S. Goldsmith, "The Christ-Prayer—Inner Communion,"
"The Second 1956 Chicago Closed Class.

Chapter Seven

Preparation for
Spiritual Baptism

Spiritual grace is an anointing by the Spirit, and our part in receiving this anointing is to prepare for it. Many persons wonder why the blessings of the Spirit do not come to them, or at least why these blessings do not come in greater measure, and yet they do not realize that they themselves are setting up the barriers that prevent it.

There is probably one thing that all mystics agree on in their presentation of the revelations of truth that have come to them, and that is that the nature of God is love. That is one outstanding agreement. To receive God is to receive love, but what do we offer as instruments through which to receive love?

The answer is that in the degree that we live as human beings, we engage in judgment, criticism, condemnation, and unforgiveness. As human beings, we live out from the old Hebraic eye-for-an-eye-and-tooth-for-a-tooth law, and are quite unable to forgive seventy times seven. In a consciousness of that nature, it is virtually impossible to receive the anointing of the Spirit. We must prepare ourselves for the anointing by a change from within which in scripture has been called the renewing of the mind: "Be ye transformed by the renewing of your mind."[1]

When the Master taught such things as loving our neighbor as ourselves, praying for the enemy, forgiving those who persecute us, resisting not evil, he was not actually setting forth a spiritual message. He was preparing human consciousness to receive the anointing of the Spirit because until we bring ourselves to that state of consciousness, to that renewal of our mind, it is not possible to receive the Holy Ghost.

The Pure Consciousness Is Free of Judgment

One example of the necessity for freedom from judgment as to what is pure and what is not pure can be found in the experience of Peter who in the depth of his great love for Judaism could not bring himself to eat the meat of the pig or to teach the truth of the Christian message to the Gentiles. The love that Peter had for the Judaic religion compelled him to feel that this great wisdom should be kept for Hebrews alone, and it also compelled him to observe the Hebraic customs, all this in the name of God, all in the name of the Christ.

Then he had a dream in which "all manner of four-footed beasts of the earth"[2] were lowered in a sheet three times and he was told to eat of them. His response was that he could not do that; "I have never eaten anything that is common or unclean."[3] When he renounced it as filthy the third time that it was offered to him, he was told to call nothing filthy that God had created. Through this symbolic experience, he saw the error of his whole philosophy and realized that he was not only refusing to eat certain meat, but he was refusing to impart truth to the Gentiles because in his mind anybody who was not a Hebrew was filthy, in other words, beyond the pale. He saw then that God had created man, all men, in His image and likeness, not just Hebrews. God created man in His image and likeness, and therefore, all men were to partake of this divine wisdom, of this spiritual meat.

Having received a purification of consciousness through

this experience, when the call came to go to Cornelius, the Gentile, to talk with him and his kinsmen, Peter responded, and this time when he spoke truth to them, the Holy Ghost descended and many received It.[4] Why? Because the Holy Ghost could flow only through a prepared and purified consciousness, one that was no longer ascribing filthiness to some and godliness to others.

A Divided Household Is Not a Pure Transparency

The Spirit cannot flow through an individual who is a house divided against itself, who is seeing both good and evil. It makes no difference whether we apply good and evil to the food we eat, or whether we apply that criterion to races, religions, or nationalities. As long as we set up a barrier in our own consciousness or permit the universal belief to do it for us, we are a divided household having good and evil, and we are not a prepared, purified consciousness through which the Spirit can flow.

Not only is it necessary that the spiritual leader or teacher be purified in consciousness, but as the patient or student goes through a process of purification, in that degree does he respond and receive the Holy Ghost. In the Bible, we read of multitudes being healed when the Master spoke, but scripture does not say that everyone in the multitudes was healed. From the few who stood by the Master when the time of persecution came, we know how few there were who received the Holy Ghost during his ministry.

We who embark on a spiritual way of life must not believe that acquiring truth is in itself sufficient to bring us the harmony, the spiritual delights, and the anointing that we expect. Knowing many statements of truth or being able to quote scripture does not necessarily constitute purification. In the message of the Infinite Way, truth has been set forth in its simplest terms. That can serve as a guide to us, but it will not be the purification, nor will it guarantee us attainment. There is no such thing as a message that will do that: it is our acceptance of the message and our practice of it that brings about the preparation of our consciousness which leads to the attainment of the goal.

States and Stages of Consciousness

In the parable of the sower,[5] the Master points out the three states of consciousness. One is the barren state in which it is of no use to plant seeds. We could pour truth into that state of consciousness from now until doomsday, and it would have no more effect than planting seeds of vegetables or flowers in barren soil. Then there is the rocky soil in which the seeds take root for a little while, but the soil is not deep enough and pure enough for the plants to flourish. They bear a little fruit, but then they die. Finally there is the fertile soil. Translated into terms of states of consciousness, the fertile soil is our own consciousness when it has been purified of its barrenness and rockiness.

Our individual consciousness is the soil. It is into that consciousness that we are pouring truth, whether by reading, hearing, or studying it. But what is the state of that consciousness? To what degree is it stony? To what degree is it fertile?

We begin with the acknowledgment that in the beginning we are barren, barren of truth and, as human beings, we are certainly barren of love. The only kind of love we know is a personal, selfish love, a nationalistic kind of love, mother love, and child love. But as our consciousness becomes purified, we begin to ask ourselves, "Why am I doing so much for my own child and ignoring the needs of the children across the tracks? Why am I doing so much for my own Red, White, and Blue and ignoring the Green, White, and Yellow?" It is only as we become unselfed that consciousness gives evidence of a greater measure of spiritual preparation.

There is in the message of the Infinite Way a simple approach that has for its purpose the transmuting and purifying of our state of consciousness, and if we are humble enough to acknowledge that as human beings we need to work with these principles and to practice them, it will then prove beneficial to us.

Working with the Principle of One Power Enriches Consciousness

There are three principles that are essential to this purification of consciousness. One is the principle of one Power. A human being is constituted of the belief in two powers: faith in two powers and fear of two powers. If we were not living in the fear of two powers, who would care who has the bomb? Who would care if it is the flu season or the polio season? The principle of one Power is the Master's teaching. This is why he could say to the man with the withered hand, "Stretch forth thine hand."[6] This is why he was able to heal the blind man: there is only one Power; there is no power holding anyone down. Open your eyes; there is no power keeping them closed.

One Power was the tremendous import of his message. It was not *using* one Power. Even at the grave of Lazarus, he did not pray to God but rather said, "Father, I thank thee that thou hast heard me. And I knew that thou hearest me always: but because of the people which stand by I said it, that they may believe that thou hast sent me."[7]

We do not have to pray. What is there to pray about? There is only one life. All that is needed is the recognition that this is the life of God, and the life of God is immortal and eternal. It cannot die, so "Lazarus, come forth."[8] He did not have to pray about that. There is only one Life, and it is Spirit; it is immortal; it is eternal.

The healing agency is the degree of our recognition of that truth. We do not have to pray to heal the mentally ill, we have to know the truth that there is only one mind. God is the mind of man. There is nothing to pray about. "Ye shall know the truth, and the truth shall make you free."[9] What truth? The truth that God is the only power, that God is the only mind of man.

Abiding in that one Power, regardless of how barren our consciousness might be at the beginning, we shall find that working consistently with that principle, refuting every appearance of power other than the one would gradually purify and enrich our consciousness, and change the outer aspect of life.

Impersonalization of Good and Evil Makes Consciousness a Transparency for the Anointing by the Spirit

A second principle is impersonalization. When we can impersonalize both good and evil, we no longer have Christians and Jews, or Protestants and Catholics. We no longer have a dozen different Hindu faiths, two or three Chinese faiths, and half a dozen Japanese faiths. Once we have learned to impersonalize, we have God as the life and mind and soul of individual man.

This is one of the most important principles in the enriching of our consciousness. It is amazing what happens once we begin to perceive that God really constitutes our being, that we are one in spiritual sonship. It does not mean that we hide our heads in the ground and believe that everybody in the world is manifesting his spiritual identity. No, if everyone were, we would not need religious teachings of any nature.

I am sure that in heaven there are no religious teachings. There is no need for any, any more than there is a need among Infinite Way students for a religion or a church. They have the truth within their consciousness. The teaching is only for the purpose of awakening them to the truth. There is no more important truth than that of impersonalization because without that step of impersonalizing evil, there is no hope whatsoever of bringing harmony into individual experience. We cannot be instruments for healing while we are personalizing evil in any way or holding individuals personally responsible for their ills, their evils, or their faults.

In our own consciousness, it must be clear that the nature of evil is absolutely impersonal, that it has its source only in the universal belief in two powers. The very moment we are able to separate it from a person in that way, our own consciousness has been purified as Peter's was when he could no longer see evil in the Gentiles or in the animals. His consciousness was a transparency then for spiritual anointing.

It is just as important, on the other hand, to impersonalize good. Many of the world's troubles have come through personalizing good, from personalizing good in Jesus alone to personalizing good in our flag, our country, our church, our religion, our household, or our family. Many of the evils in the world are bound up in the belief that we have a monopoly of good.

Generalizations About Nations of People Are Always Incorrect

Once we learn to impersonalize, we realize that the only good there is, is God and wherever It finds an outlet, there It is in expression, and where It does not find an outlet, there It is not. We soon learn, more especially if we travel, that there is no such thing as evil races or evil peoples on earth. There may be evil individuals. But the minute we think that there are no persons who permit themselves to be instruments for evil or the carnal mind in your land or my land, we are in a state of delusion. The evil is anywhere and everywhere God is not recognized as the source of good.

Good is everywhere. So it is that as far as people are concerned, we find good people in every nation and we also find a percentage of bad ones, and probably the same percentage in all nations. It has nothing to do with one's nationality, race, or religion. It has to do with an individual's degree of purified consciousness.

When at sixteen and a half years, I started traveling the world, it did not take me very long to discover that the English people were good, just as good as we were, and the French, the German, and the Swiss. It did not take me long, also, to find that there were dishonest ones among all of them and that there were business people one could not trust. No one country, however, had a monopoly on them. So it was that as a young man, I saw that humanly there is no such thing anywhere as good people as a race or bad people as a race. They are what they are as individuals, what their state of consciousness is.

Only later when the spiritual experience began, did I understand why this is inevitably true. God is the underlying life of every individual; God is the mind, the Spirit, and the soul of everyone. Therefore, the foundation of every one of us is the same.

Furthermore, because the carnal mind is one, the carnal mind in every one of us is the same: every nation has its bigots; every nation has the cruel; every nation has the miserly; every nation has the tyrant. This must inevitably be because the carnal mind, the belief in good and evil, is what constitutes those qualities, and so wherever the carnal mind is, we are going to find those who appear as evil. Let us not think the carnal mind is something separate and apart from churches, governments, and people, because the carnal mind is one, and wherever there is a receptivity to the carnal mind, it finds expression.

Heretofore, the world has had no opportunity of freeing itself from this carnal mind. It was believed that we had to go out and reform every individual on earth separately and individually, that we had to proselyte and work with individuals and bring them all into our way of life. This belief would make the world situation hopeless because by the time we could get around to the four billion people on earth and reform all of them, the next generation would be here and we would have to begin our work all over again. That is the only hope that has been held out up to now. But now we know that it is not going to be necessary to reform four billion people; it is not going to be necessary to make four billion people spiritual or even to make them want to be spiritual or to have a need for it. Now the "ten"[10] righteous men in the city that are going to save it are the few who are going to be able to impersonalize and nothingize the carnal mind.

We impersonalize evil so that we understand that evil is not Christian, Jewish, or Moslem. We impersonalize evil so that we know that evil is not our neighbor down the street or somebody else. We recognize that we are dealing only with the carnal mind, and the carnal mind can appear as white or black, Jew or Gentile. Once we have impersonalized it and separated it from a person and recognized it as the carnal mind, we can then take the third step of nothingizing it by realizing that God did not create the carnal mind: it has no entity or identity, no substance, no law, no cause, no effect.

Casting Out the Stones

When we work with these three principles—one Power, the impersonalization of good and evil, and the nothingization of the carnal mind, we are enriching consciousness. We are throwing the stones out of the stony soil; we are getting rid of the rocks which are the barriers to spiritual realization. We are feeding our consciousness with spiritual food and enriching the barren soil.

It is all a matter of our knowing the truth, loving our neighbor, praying for those who persecute us, forgiving seventy times seven, and resisting not evil. It is not that there is some kind of a super-being or force that is going to come down to us and make us all over. Even those who have had the experience of

Grace have spent years afterward understanding its meaning and bringing out the fruitage. Paul spent nine years after his experience of Light before he was ready to go forth, and, even after the disciples had spent three years with him, the Master discouraged them from rushing out and instructed them to remain in the city until they were empowered from on High.

After we receive the Light, it takes a long time to convert that into a practical fertile consciousness. Even after we know this truth of one Power, of impersonalizing good and evil, and of nothingizing the carnal mind, let us not think for a moment that we are immediately going to be able to go out and live it. We still have remnants of that old human consciousness that judges, criticizes, condemns, and divides.

After this truth is given us, it has to be worked with, it has to be utilized, it has to be put into practice, and by this process we feed our consciousness with truth and thereby enrich the soil, remove the stones, and prepare ourselves for a spiritual anointing. That is why in the guru system of teaching, the disciple or student is with the teacher for a number of years. Why a number of years? Why does not the *guru* give the disciple the truth at once? It would do no good. A consciousness of truth has to be built; spiritual consciousness has to be developed.

If a person had a religious experience or experienced the Light and did not know what to do with it afterward, he would be like many of those described by Dr. Bucke in *Cosmic Consciousness*. Hundreds who had deep spiritual experiences reported that they lived miserable lives thereafter because they could not bring that experience about again. They did not know what to do with it or how to live it. Had they but known how to keep their experience locked up within themselves and then receive instruction from within and to apply it, the experience would have been only the beginning of their great spiritual conversion.

So it is with us. We are too likely to believe after we have read a few books of truth that we really know something, and the next thing is that we are expecting miracles to happen. Miracles do happen but they come out of an attained spiritual consciousness, not out of a knowledge of truth. Miracles are happening every day of the week, but the miracles take place because of the purified consciousness, the prepared consciousness. They do not happen because of a book we have read; they do not happen because we know the Bible; they do not happen because of a teaching we have or a teacher: they happen because of what happens within us with the teaching or with the teacher.

Purification, a Requisite for Spiritual Anointing

We have the opportunity to bring about a purification of our consciousness, which is the preparation for a spiritual anointing. First, we must recognize that a spiritual anointing can come only to the consciousness that is prepared for it. This preparation consists of the degree of spiritual vision which we attain. The practice of it is in the degree that we live with one Power, the degree that we impersonalize both good and evil, and nothingize them. In this degree, are we purifying our consciousness as Peter was purified in that dream-experience.

Every step of our journey on this path is one of purification. Sometimes we have to get very hard knocks before we will accept purification, and there is a natural reason for this for which no one should be condemned, but which should be understood. It is so comfortable to have a healthy body and a sufficiency of income that the nature of the spiritual universe does not then arouse any interest, much less concern. Why concern ourselves now with that which is so difficult to attain?

It is natural to rejoice in material good and to enjoy living in the midst of it. This is the reason that very often the props are knocked out from under us and everything that has supported us in the past is taken away from us, everything on which we have had reliance. Many is the time a disciple has cried out, "You have taken my God away from me." This is a step forward in consciousness because there is no healthier experience in the world than losing one's faith in God.

As a matter of fact, until one loses faith in one's God, how is one to find the true God? As long as a person has faith in a God from which there is no fruitage, he has not found the true God. He is entertaining a false concept of God and he wants to cling to it as Peter wanted to cling to his Hebraic God. This was true of the other disciples as well. It took Paul, who was not an immediate disciple of Jesus, to awaken them out of that particular state of consciousness.

Becoming Free of Concepts of God

Who knows what particular event in our experience will awaken us to the fact that we have not been worshiping God, but have been entertaining a false concept of God and expecting it to do certain things for us in a certain way, and it has not done this. We have not found God. We have been entertaining a concept of God, and until that concept is taken from us, until we lose our faith in that God, just as Jesus made His followers lose faith in all the things in which they had their reliance, we will not find God.

The Hebrew people in the days of the Master were worshiping and placing power in the forms—the rituals, the sacrifices, all the things that were meant to take them into heaven—and finally Jesus had to tell them that their faith had to be greater than that of the scribes and the Pharisees, their purity, their religion had to be greater than that. There was none greater than the scribes and the Pharisees. They lived up to every law, never violating a decree of the church, and yet the righteousness of the disciples had to be greater than that. What greater is there? First of all, they had to unlearn everything the scribes and the Pharisees knew. They had to learn that obeying laws and going through rituals, ceremonies, rites, and creeds had no relationship at all to the true God. Going to the holy temple once a year did not cleanse or purify a person.

God is not on a throne up in the clouds: the kingdom of God is within; God has no pleasure in sacrifice; God does not sentence a thief to be crucified on the cross or sent to prison forever. Criminals are not to be punished but forgiven. This does not mean that they are to be turned loose to commit more crimes. Reformation and instruction should become the goal in dealing with criminals. Some day prisons will be set up to achieve that objective.

Today there are some prisons for moral offenders that are not really prisons: there are no bars and no walls. They are hospitals to which the convicted persons are sent, not for punishment but for treatment. Punishment does not change the nature of a thief, nor does it cure a thief. One day thieves will be sentenced to prison for the purpose of regeneration, education, spiritual and cultural training in order to change their consciousness from barren and rocky soil to fertile soil for the planting of spiritual truth.

In a measure, our human consciousness is that carnal mind. Whether or not we are ever convicted of a crime does not mean that we are not guilty of one or more. It means that we have not been caught, or that the degree is not quite the same, but the carnal mind is the carnal mind whether it is in you or me, or the criminal. It operates in the same way.

Preparation for Anointing Through a Practice of the Principles

Preparation for the anointing of the Spirit takes place within us. We have it within ourselves to hasten that day, not because we can take heaven by force, but because we can make of every day an opportunity for consciously remembering that we are to live in the realization of one Power, that we are to impersonalize every form of good or evil we behold or read or hear on the radio or on television as the carnal mind and nothingize it. As we do this, we can be assured that we are enriching the soil of our consciousness. We are removing those rocks that are barriers and are preparing ourselves for spiritual anointing.

Spiritual anointing eventually comes as it did to Paul, and yet that influx of the Spirit was only a step that prepared him for that final anointing, which did not come until he was ready to be sent out on his mission. Peter, too, must have had many spiritual anointings, but his real anointing came only with that dream in which he saw that everything that God made is good so there is only one Power, and he also saw that good and evil must be impersonal.

So it is that the first touch of the Spirit may be our first anointing. It is not our final one, and there will not be a final one, unless we take advantage of the first one and work with it and allow its lesson to become settled within us and then applied in our daily experience.

Impersonalization, the Razor's Edge

It seems very difficult at times to walk the razor's edge. It is not easy to know when we are impersonalizing and yet not being imposed upon, by which I mean, when we can impersonalize the evil in the thief and yet not set him free to do it all over again, when we can behold the impersonal nature of evil and still have our feet on the ground enough to be able to correct ourselves and others, especially the others who are entrusted to us for spiritual teaching until they, too, have realized the impersonal nature of good and evil.

Sometimes it is said that we are inconsistent when we talk

about the impersonal nature of evil and then correct somebody. It must be understood that in this work we correct only those who have come to us for spiritual instruction, and that correction is not denying the impersonal nature of the evil, but helping the student to come to the realization and demonstration of it, not being satisfied merely to quote it but to insist on its demonstration.

"Ye have not chosen me, but I have chosen you."[11] There are no persons who remain on the spiritual path, in spite of many upsets, who will not ultimately attain, because it is not they who brought themselves to it. They were pushed into it in spite of themselves. They are going to be kept on it until the day of anointing comes. There are many, of course, who come to a spiritual teaching who have really not been chosen. They come for the loaves and the fishes. They come because they have heard that this is the way they can be healed or enriched or have some other thing come to them. When they find that this is not always true, that healings do not always happen in a hurry, that riches do not always come rapidly, that personal happiness does not always come in the form they expect, they drop away. But they were not seeking It, only the fruitage of It.

There are many who do not receive their blessings early in their experience and yet they persist and persist and persist. They get knocked down and get up again. They are brushed aside and pull themselves up again. There is a reason for this persistence in the face of great odds. The seed has been planted; the *I* has called to them, and in one way or another It is going to bring them home. Sometimes in order to bring a person home, severe trials and temptations come to him over and over again.

A Call To Aid in the Solution of World Problems Comes to the Anointed

When we are on the spiritual path and have received a measure of Light, even though we may be free of major personal problems and the great trials and tribulations of humanhood, we are faced with the temptations of this world. The Master said that he could pick up his life or lay it down. He did not have to stay there to be crucified. He went through that experience for the sake of the world, for the message and the mission given to him. For his own personal sake, he could have walked right through the crowds and walked away; he could have moved to a cabin by the sea and lived. But the inner drive would not permit that, and therefore he had to overcome the world in order that the rest of us could benefit by his experience.

So it is when the time comes that we receive our release from this world and are no longer touched by major problems, we shall find then that we have our hardest task because we have the entire world, the whole of the carnal mind, presenting itself to us to be met. We cannot take the measure of truth that we have received and withdraw from the world and say, "Now, World, you bear yourself up if you want to."

Every one of us on this path is being faced with nuclear warfare and all the other world problems. Can we think for a moment that these are not your problems and mine? They are more our problems than they are those of the heads of governments who are only finite men with no wisdom beyond their human ability to solve any of these problems. None of these men has the capacity to solve them. None of them in the past fifty years has had the answer to any of these problems.

These world problems are yours and mine because they are spiritual problems, that is, they are problems that have to be solved spiritually. If we do not undertake to see that what is being presented to us as problems in the form of Communism, Apartheid, Indo-China, or Berlin is only the carnal mind in different forms, who can meet them? Who except those who know how to impersonalize and nothingize? Does anyone else have the answer? Of course not, because no one has solved these pressing problems of human life.

The only real advance that has been made in the last two thousand years has been in the area of mechanization. We have developed mechanically, and the very machines that have been invented are helping to destroy the world. It is not only the atomic bomb. The automobile and the airplane are causing as many deaths as anything else.

Those who are personalizing evil and who are believing that it is a force and power are never going to eradicate it. They do not have the answer because the answer lies in Spirit, in Truth, and that means that the answer lies in recognizing one Power, impersonalizing, and nothingizing.

At first, we cannot see that our function or our mission in life is not just to be healthy, wealthy, and wise, and acquire a nice comfortable form of living. That is not our mission in life. Our mission is to be spiritually anointed and then to take that anointing out into the world, out into the carnal mind, dissolving the carnal mind that the spiritual universe may be revealed here and now. The way to do it has been given to us: one Power, impersonalize good and evil, nothingize the carnal mind.

Every time we bring these principles even to the healing of a headache, a cold, the flu, a corn, a bunion, or indigestion, in that degree we have lessened it in the world. Every time we go further and can witness the dissolution of a cancer, polio, or any one of these so-called incurable diseases, we have further lessened the activity of the carnal mind. Every time we can bring a measure of peace to a governmental agency, a commercial firm, an educational system, every time we can bring one iota of spiritual Grace to these, we have lessened the carnal mind activity throughout the world.

Let us never believe when an individual is healed spiritually that it is only the individual who is healed: the carnal mind has been lessened; more of Christhood has been revealed on earth. Healing is not removing disease from the human being; it is revealing his Christhood, and that can come about only through the destruction of the carnal mind. The destruction of the carnal mind comes only through the understanding of one Power, impersonalization, nothingization. The practice of these principles brings the purification that is the preparation for the anointing.

Chapter Eight

The Fourth Dimension

There are two types of religious life. One is the life of those whose religion consists in following certain rituals, observing holy days and feast days, and going through the forms of certain prayers. With this they are satisfied. They have approached or reached a state of consciousness which is at peace because they are doing what is expected of them and what is right in their eyes. They have little idea of the real meaning of religion or of God, but merely accept what is presented to them and abide in that.

The other type of religious life is the one that has no set rules or regulations. As a matter of fact, it has no chart to guide anyone in his search, but is really the soul of an individual seeking to find rest in God and to find its spiritual home.

There is one thing alone that makes us human beings. Except for that one thing, even as we are, here in our bodies, we would not be human beings; we would be divine, immortal, eternal. That one thing is that we entertain a sense of separation from God. In reality, we are not separated from God: we are one with God. As a matter of fact, God constitutes our very being; and therefore, we are immortal being right now. Through this sense of separation, however, we have built up an identity of our own. It is this that constitutes our humanhood, and emerging out of that humanhood into a realization of our true identity is the work of the spiritual path.

The Soul-Center Seeks
Conscious Union With Its Source

Within us is this that we call the soul, and you do not know what the soul is any more than I do. It is merely a word that is used to describe our spiritual center, that part of our consciousness which embodies our religious life. Just as there is a center of our being which is our artistic or musical center, a center of our consciousness which constitutes our business ability or acumen, and a center which responds to science, there is also a center of our being which responds to the religious or spiritual impulse. We call that part of us our soul.

This soul is within us, but not within the body, not even within consciousness, for in the last analysis the soul constitutes our consciousness. But, since I am *I*, there is an area of my being which is my soul-center, and that soul-center is seeking conscious union with its source. Through my entertaining a sense of separation from God, it is as if I were holding this soul-center outside of God and keeping it away from its union with God. It is almost as if we were to say, "Here is a ray of sunshine separated from the sun and aching to get back there."

This soul-center is in the midst of each of us, within our own consciousness, but as human beings it is cut off from the Father. In an absolute spiritual sense, it is not cut off, but it appears to be because of our entertaining this sense of separation. Therefore it seems to us as if something within us is driving us on to seek something that we do not have.

The person who does not have a sufficiency of supply may believe that that drive within him is to gain more supply. That is why there are persons in this world who never rest until they get their first million, and then they get their second wind to go after that second, fifth, or tenth million. There are persons who long to be presidents and prime ministers, and when they attain that and get their second wind, they are ready for the next term and the next term. They cannot be satisfied because there is a drive within them, stemming from their own sense of incompleteness. They interpret this incompleteness and lack of satisfaction as meaning, "I must get there. I must attain. I must achieve." They do not realize what it is that is working in them, and so they go after the thing that they can most readily understand, which at one stage may be money, honor, or fame. If they but knew, it is their soul, aching, reaching out to find its home in God, to get back into conscious union with God.

Those of us who do not feel a drive for money, fame, or attainment of any kind in the world recognize what it is that is driving us. We know that we are never going to be satisfied until we find ourselves at home in Him, and it is this drive that brings us to where we are at this particular minute. We know that we are never going to have rest until we come face to face with God, until we realize consciously that the spirit of God within us is the very life and soul of our being and that we can commune with It. In fact, we can commune with our inner being even more easily than we can commune with one another.

There are those students who do not know that what is driving them on is the soul itself trying to break through this veil of illusion and once more attain union with God, and they are driven by the belief that they must find health or that they must find supply. Sometimes they find health and supply very quickly, and that delays their spiritual progress for many years, because now, having no further incentive, they rest back in their health or in their supply, until years later they probably come into the realization, "Well, now I have my health and my supply, but I am still unhappy. I am still longing for something"; or,

"I have a happy home, and still I am yearning for something." And probably at that period they may begin to awaken to the fact that if they have all the health in the world, all the wealth in the world, and the happiest home in the world, they still will not be at peace until they find themselves home in God.

Students Have Nothing To Impart
Without the Anointing of the Spirit

There is a second stage on the path, which is a dangerous one. That is when the student has attained some measure of health and some easing of the supply situation, and then wants to begin to give to others what he has learned. This is a dangerous period because, if he is not stopped, he will find some way to go ahead and mount up on a platform and begin to teach. In doing this, he will find that he has lost everything that he had gained, and he will find it even more difficult to get back on the path than were the first steps he took in that direction.

The reason that a student should be wary when he reaches this stage is that no one has anything to impart of a spiritual nature, except the spirit of God has come upon him, ordained him, and sent him out into the world and given him his work to do. Most students in the metaphysical and spiritual world do not wait for that anointing. They do not wait for that experience of the Christ. They go out and soon find that even though they may have started out with very large groups, they end up with small ones; or, if they have started out with small groups, they do not increase.

Human beings have nothing to give spiritually, not a thing. Even if they know all the scriptures of the world, they still have nothing to give; and if they have received the ordination of the greatest churches of the world, still they have nothing to give. It makes no difference how much they know, whether of scripture, metaphysics, or of mysticism; they still are spiritually barren and they have nothing to impart. If they could impart the letter of truth that they know, even if they could impart it correctly, it still would be of no value to anyone else. It is only in the degree in which the Spirit works through an individual that the letter of truth becomes the spirit of truth, and brings the student alive. In the Master's words, "And I, if I be lifted up from the earth, will draw all men unto me."[1]

Good Humanhood Is Not Related to Spiritual Attainment

The world is full of good men and women. This has nothing to do with a spiritual equation, however, and it has nothing to do with a spiritual ministry. As a matter of fact, some of the greatest spiritual lights of the world were not among the best of human beings when they began.

Sometimes being a very good human being is a barrier to being a spiritual light, because it takes a great deal of humility to attain spiritual realization. The first step in that humility is when the recognition comes that man can be neither good nor evil. That is a very difficult thing for good human beings to accept. They love to dwell on their own goodness and to feel that it is a virtue for which they are entitled to great credit.

Furthermore, good human beings are very prone to criticize, judge, or condemn the sinner, or the one who is somewhat less perfect than themselves. Right there they create a block through which the spirit of God cannot penetrate. It is true that God's rain falls on the just and the unjust. It is true that the Master held no one in condemnation. To him there was no waiting for punishment, no waiting to be purged, no waiting for forgiveness.

It takes a great deal of humility for a good person to recognize that he is not good but that whatever goodness is manifested in him is really the spirit of God trying to find outlet. If

that were more clearly understood, we could then more right-
fully enjoy goodness by realizing, "This is not my goodness.
This is the goodness of God finding an outlet through me. It is
not that I am generous, but that God's gift is being sent out into
circulation through me."

With such an attitude, we understand more readily the person who for any reason or in any way has fallen from Grace or
is away from the path of Grace, because it is only the belief that
that individual of himself can be good or bad, and at this particular moment being bad seems the most satisfactory way or
the most profitable one.

The Remnant,
Those Who Attain Conscious Union

Those who are seriously directed to the spiritual path
should understand that their work at this moment is not to concern themselves with trying to save the world or even their relatives, but first of all with being saved themselves. This may
sound selfish, but it is the very opposite of selfishness. Our primary function is to be concerned with only one thing, and that
is that we attain conscious union with God. The rest of the
world may have to battle out their woes by themselves while we
stand by. We have to keep right on seeking the kingdom of God,
seeking to attain our conscious union with God. If meanwhile
the world swallows itself up, we cannot help it. It has always
been that way.

There have been many civilizations destroyed in the past,
and there are going to be quite a few destroyed from here on,
but there has always been a remnant of those who were saved
when civilizations were destroyed. Always after that destruction
there were the few, who not only were saved, but left a record
that helped save those of future generations. So it is that the
Bible, the scriptures of all peoples and the mystical writings of

all nations, these are the things that are helping you and me right now.

A Developed Spiritual Consciousness Functions Eternally

We are helped by those who have passed from our sight. Never believe that there is a retrograde step from developed spiritual consciousness. If an individual attains spiritual consciousness on earth, he is a blessing to everyone who brings himself within range of his consciousness and even to some who are not aware of what is going on. But when that individual leaves this human plane of life, his spiritually developed consciousness continues on just the same. It cannot be put into a grave. Those who have meditated with the *I* know:

> I was never born and I will never die.
> That I was never confined in a physical body,
> much less will I ever be confined in a tomb.

> "I and my Father are one,"[2] and therefore I am never
> limited to time, space, or place. I and the Father
> within are one, and that One is immortal. Therefore
> I go on forever and forever and forever. That I which
> I am is the state of consciousness which I am.

So if anyone is benefitting by our developed state of consciousness here and now on earth, we can be assured that those same benefits will be going on throughout eternity. If we believe that Jesus Christ was the great light that he was and that his three years in the ministry could produce the effect on the world for twenty centuries that it has and believe that it came to an end on that cross or in that tomb, we have not thought deeply enough. That degree of consciousness which we know as Christ

Jesus could never come to an end. There would be something wrong with God if such a light could pass from existence or be withdrawn from the world.

I say this also of Gautama the Buddha. If, at his state of elevation, his consciousness could be nullified, there is no justice in the divine kingdom. That state of development or any state leading up to it is perpetual. It is eternal and it is forever a transparency through which God reaches this earth, and that is what accounts for the individuals on earth who attain spiritual light.

Think of a man, a cobbler by trade, with no greater religious teaching or thought than a darkened theological background, living at a time of tremendous blackness, of spiritual ignorance personified; think of that man in one second receiving such light that within a couple of years he was known from Switzerland to England as the greatest spiritual teacher on earth. He became the teacher of several generations of mystics, and to this very day, the writings he left behind are read by so many hundreds of thousands of people in the world that editions are continually being published in England and in the United States. That man we all recognize as Jacob Boehme of Germany. Today there is not a religious teaching in the world that does not know and honor him. That could not have been an accident. It could not have been anything other than that the illumined consciousness of someone touched him. It may have been one of those who had passed on or it may have been one on earth.

Infinite Consciousness Is Never Locked Up in a Body

When we pray, when we commune with God, we are at-one with all men and all women who are praying. We are at-one with spiritual consciousness throughout this world and the worlds that have been and the worlds that will be. We are never alone because there is no such thing as our consciousness being locked up in our head, in our chest, or in our solar plexus. Our consciousness fills all space; that is the nature of *I*. It cannot be localized or "finitized" for that is an infinite relationship with infinite Being.

The moment we understand that our consciousness is not locked up inside of us, but that it is one with everyone we know, then eventually we will go further, and we will realize that when we are in prayer, we are in attunement with everyone in prayer because we are uniting in the one Consciousness. The Christ-consciousness is one Consciousness, and when we are abiding in that, we are abiding in Christ.

The error has been that we have believed we are finite beings sitting in a body. This is not true: we are infinite being; we are divine Consciousness, God-consciousness individualized, but never finitized and never localized. Therefore, we are never limited to a place. We are where we want to be merely in this realization:

> I and the Father are one:
> I am where God is, and God is where I am.

Then we will find ourselves where harmony is for us at any given moment.

On our pathway upward to that realization, many of us are being fed by the life, the message, and the mission of Jesus Christ. Some are being fed by the life of Buddha, Lao-tze, or the original great master of Zen. Some are being fed in this very age by the writings of Ralph Waldo Emerson, Walt Whitman, William Law, Eckhart, Boehme, and all the rest of these. Many millions are being fed by the works of Mary Baker Eddy. So is it not clear that, regardless of what happens in this world, there is a remnant that is saved and there are always, one, two, three, four, five, or six in every generation who, having caught this light, leave either an oral or a written message? Even without leaving a written message, the Master was able to say, "My

words shall not pass away."[3] The earth may crumble, as it has
many, many times since he left here, but "my words," the words
of the Master Jesus, will keep on saving this world until it is
completely saved. So it may also be said of these other mystics.

We, too, are transparencies through which this transcendental Presence can function in the consciousness of this world.
In our world prayer work, when we are thinking of those in this
world who are being handled by evil, those who are letting
themselves be outlets for evil, we realize, " 'Father, forgive them;
for they know not what they do.'[4] Hold them not in condemnation, but open their consciousness to this light that they may
be freed of this temptation, of this hypnotism, or of whatever it
is that binds them to personal sense." With that, there is the
removal of condemnation from them, because we have declared
that it is not sin, it is merely ignorance; it is not darkness, but
an absence of light.

We have no way of knowing how the Light, which reaches
the earth through the transparency of those in prayer, influences
legislation or how It changes decisions. We never know where
this Presence that we have realized touches or whom It touches.
We have no idea how far reaching It is. That is why some who
have attained the Light retire from this world in order to live the
life of prayer for the world, not for individuals but for the breaking down of the human consciousness of duality. By remaining
in their caves or in their little houses somewhere alone, they
permit themselves, by praying without ceasing, to be transparencies through which the Light comes and they have no way
of knowing who is touched by It or how.

It is evident that things do happen on earth that cannot be
accounted for. There are people in hospitals about to die who
suddenly find themselves well, and no one has the slightest idea
of how it happened. There are times when countries are at the
brink of war, and at the last minute a decision changes it. It is
not always a human thing that brought about the change.

Attainment Comes Only When
the Spirit of God Dwells in Us

If a person on the path could be as patient as was Buddha, who waited twenty-one years to receive his illumination, or as the Master, who began his ministry at the age of thirty, after having been engaged in this study perhaps from the age of six or eight or nine, if he could be that patient to wait for his own fulfillment, then would he become the light of the world. But if a person does not have that Light, just having a knowledge of what is in books will not help him. The books of the Infinite Way serve as inspiration and guidance, as path-finders or maps, just as do the writings of all these other Masters, but the task of arriving, that is the person's own responsibility.

We have not arrived until the spirit of God dwells in us, until we can say with Paul, "I live; yet not I, but Christ liveth in me."[5]

> Christ is living my life: Christ goes before me to make my way straight; Christ walks beside me; Christ walks behind me; Christ envelops me. I am enfolded in the Christ. " The spirit of the Lord God is upon me; because he hath anointed me." [6]
>
> Christ is the bread, and the wine, and the water. Christ does not resurrect me; Christ is the resurrection.

The spirit of God is the resurrection. "But if the Spirit of him that raised up Jesus from the dead dwell in you, he that raised up Christ from the dead shall also quicken your mortal bodies by his Spirit that dwelleth in you."[7] Why? Because the realization of the Christ is the resurrection of the body—the raising of it out of the tomb of human belief.

Living the Life of "Resist Not Evil"

On all sides today it is said that it is impossible to live the teachings of Jesus Christ in this life. One of the reasons it seems impossible to most persons stems primarily from Jesus' statement, "Resist not evil."[8] In this age, it would seem that if we do not resist evil, evil will do something terrible to us. Of course, the record of thousands of years shows how religiously the world has resisted evil, with everything from bows and arrows to atomic bombs. And with all this resistance, from what has it been saved? Not a thing.

We have been resisting evil until now we have warehouses full of the greatest arsenal of weapons the world has ever known. And the fear is just as great; the anxiety is just as great.

Resisting evil has proved to be a failure. Those who say that it is not practical to live without resisting evil have not tried it. Everyone who, at some time or other, has asked for metaphysical or spiritual help without resorting to the use of *materia medica* has had proof that not resisting evil is the great power. If a person is ill and he reaches out for every and any material remedy that is at hand, he is resisting the evil. But those who have had healings through spiritual means have had the proof of what can happen by not resisting evil.

The spiritual practitioner has no way to fight the evil, whether the evil is a fever, a growth, wasting away, or broken bones. With him, there can be no reliance on any physical means. His consciousness is a state of absolute and complete surrender to the inner conviction that since God is the one power, we need not fear any other power, and we can rest in that word. That is the kind of treatment that heals. We cannot battle error, whether it is physical evil, mental evil, moral evil, or financial evil. We cannot battle it. The people of the world are battling it, but we could hardly call what they have accomplished success. Practically all the diplomats and leaders of the world have been incapable of keeping their countries out of war because they have built on the false foundation of resisting evil. The world today is paying the penalty for their error.

Probably the day may come when some of us will be given the opportunity to prove that this principle operates nationally and internationally, the same as it operates in the healing of our minds, our bodies, and our pocketbooks individually. It is for this reason that I say that no one should go out into the world to teach or preach this. Stay at home and demonstrate it, and let the world behold it. In proportion as the world beholds it, it will want to learn what it is that we have and will then invite us to tell about it. That will be the time to tell, to teach, to preach, and not until then.

Discover the Meaning of "My Peace" and "My Kingdom"

To what degree are we basing our spiritual demonstration on "My peace I give unto you"[9] and "My kingdom is not of this world"[10]? To what extent are we expecting that through God we will have more of the peace that this world can give: physical health, material supply, a comfortable home, human companionship? To what extent are we expecting the kingdom of God to increase the degree of our human comfort? Then we will see, perhaps, where we have been amiss, where we are living in the theology of the Old Testament, believing that if we pray, tithe, sacrifice, or observe the holy days God will do something to make our human life better. To what extent are we living in that Old Testament belief?

To what extent are we expecting something from God, attempting to influence God, or hoping to set aside some law of God? In our praying, are we actually believing that God is withholding something but that after this prayer it will be granted? Are we reaching up to God or are we resting in the realization of this inner communion? Is our prayer a realization of God's presence?

In one way or another, our prayer should be the realization that we are one with the Father and that the Lord is our shepherd. Our prayer should always remain on that level where it is not reaching up or out or within for something. Prayer in its highest sense has no words and no thoughts: it is merely an inner communion that becomes a oneness, a union with God, a resting in God. Then we become clear transparencies through which God's grace touches the consciousness of all those who are reaching out to us.

To come out and be separate, to leave our nets, not increase the catch in them, but to leave them means to give up and surrender the idea of increasing the amount of the peace of this world that we can get, and see to what extent we can base our demonstration on seeking not the peace that this world can give, but seeking to know what the kingdom of God consists of. What is the meaning of *My* peace? What is the meaning of *My* kingdom? *My* peace and *My* kingdom have no relationship to improving or increasing matter. They have to do with an entirely different world, a fourth dimension of life.

It is true and it is a promise of the Master that if we seek this particular Kingdom, the things of this world will be added unto us, not by virtue of our seeking them, but by virtue of our surrendering the seeking of them and devoting ourselves to the seeking of *My* peace and *My* kingdom.

To move from the Hebraic state of consciousness to the Christian means to make a transition from seeking to improve our "this world" to giving up all of this world for *My* sake— mother, brother, father, sister—whatever human concepts we have of good. We give up the human concept of what a good neighbor is, because even a good neighbor at his best is not good. But what is neighbor in the sense that Jesus meant when he said, "Love thy neighbor as thyself"?[11]

The New Testament consists of a whole new language. It

says, "They shall speak with new tongues,"[12] a new language, words that do not have the same meaning as the dictionary gives. To come fully into the spiritual way of life means to understand these new tongues, this new language, and no longer to be hypnotized by the good of this world, but to loose it and let it go, to leave our nets, and turn within silently, secretly, sacredly, telling nobody what we are doing, but pounding away at the gates of our own consciousness until it reveals to us the hidden meaning of the Master's message.

In the New Dimension All Things Are Provided

Then as realization comes, we will find that we are living in a new dimension of life. We will not have sacrificed anything of this world—not a thing. All the *things* of this world will be added unto us, but with this difference: by that time we will not appreciate them too much. We will just use them for their utilitarian value.

There are those who will come to us, not knowing anything of this new Kingdom, but seeking to improve their humanhood, and we must help them. That is the first stage of their entrance to the path. The second stage is when they begin to learn the words and have a do-gooder complex, and want to rush out and save the world. Then we must use our influence to halt them and tell them to wait patiently until the spirit of the Lord God is upon them, and then, if necessary, they could go out without money, without food, without clothing. They could start right out and find that at every step of the way, if manna were needed it would come from the sky, if water were needed it would come from a rock, if clothing were needed that which they had on would never wear out. In other words, God would not provide: God would *be* their safety and security. God would not feed them: God itself would be their food.

When we have attained the presence of God, we have

attained the presence of every blessed thing that one may need in a journey through this life.

ACROSS THE DESK

Infinite Way students around the world rejoice as they see the Infinite Way gaining more and more recognition and an ever-greater number of persons being drawn to its message. Many of these new students have found the Infinite Way through the books that have been placed in libraries by students who were led to do this. Now the Infinite Way library activity is being carried on by two dedicated students who years ago on their own initiative and originally at their own expense began sending out books on a wide scale to theological seminaries requesting them. The support of this activity by students will help it to continue and will provide an opportunity for all those students who participate to practice the principle of impersonal giving.

Almost a year ago in the *United States News and World Report,* September 20, 1971, a full page editorial by David Lawrence gave recognition to one of Joel's books: *Living the Infinite Way.* We are grateful to this highly respected writer for calling this book to the attention of the readers of such a widely circulated and well-established magazine.

Another interesting item is an article on meditation that appeared in *The Cleveland Press,* October 30, 1971, in which there is a photograph of Joel and a quotation under the title "Western-Style Meditation: How and Why It Works." On the same page in a much longer article, "How To Get What You Want Without Asking," there is the following quotation from Joel:

"Our culture has focused attention on the things of the world to such an extent that we have lost the capacity to sit quietly and ponder an idea. When we close our eyes to meditate, we are amazed to discover a boiler factory within us. We are like antennas picking up all the broadcasts of the world."

The above examples are evidence of the Spirit working in and as individual consciousness, opening whatever doors need to be opened to bring the Infinite Way to the awareness of those who are seeking a satisfying, new, and rewarding approach to life.

Tape Recorded Excerpts
Prepared by the Editor

Attaining the Spiritual Kingdom

"Once you rise above the desire for physical harmony, then you are entering the spiritual kingdom of God. As long as your thought is on exchanging your discords for harmonies, which it has been in metaphysics, you still have traveled only part of the journey. That journey is really not one of going from physical discord to physical harmony. . . . That is only part way along the road because all you have done is to rise above your temporary discords into temporary harmonies, but you have not achieved the realization of the spiritual kingdom. It does not yet appear what the glories of God are.

"No, as long as you are exchanging physical discord for physical harmony, you still have no idea what the kingdom of God is like or what the spiritual riches are like or even spiritual health. You have no idea of it. Just the fact that the heart beats regularly or that the organs function as what the world calls normal gives no impression of what spiritual harmony is like. None at all. It is only when you rise above physical harmony that you begin to enter the spiritual realm."

Joel S. Goldsmith, "Cosmic Law and the Realized Christ," *The 1955 First Kailua Study Group.*

Chapter Nine

From Humanhood to Divinity

The Old Testament and the New Testament together make up what the world knows as the Christian Bible, and this might lead one to think that the whole of the Old Testament is the same in its religious teaching as is the New Testament, or that in the Bible there is to be found only one teaching. This is not true.

In the Old Testament, which of course stands firmly on the teaching of Moses and the Hebrew prophets, the law is set forth. This law is the foundation for that state of our consciousness which may be called the Hebraic state, and while we are in the Hebraic state of consciousness, it is necessary to have that law.

The Law

Let us not think, however, that that is the same teaching as Christianity, or that it represents what Jesus Christ came to give this world. It does not, "for the law was given by Moses, but grace and truth came by Jesus Christ."[1] The Christian way of life is a life by grace, not a life by law. According to the teachings of Jesus Christ, we do not honor our mother and father because of obedience to one of the Ten Commandments: we honor our mother and father because we have accepted the teaching of love-thy-neighbor-as-thyself, and our mother and father are just as much a neighbor as the person down the street. It would be difficult to exclude our mother and father from our love; but, on the other hand, it should be equally difficult to exclude the neighbor down the street or across the boundary.

What do we have when we live under the law? We have a Sabbath, one day that must be kept holy. In the Christian Church, this is still observed, even though it is a different Sabbath Day from that observed in the traditional Hebrew synagogue. But anyone who sets aside any day of the week as holy or accepts one day of the week as more holy than another has not yet discerned the teaching of Jesus Christ. There are 365 holy days in every year, except Leap Year, and then there are 366 holy days. If that is not true, then Christianity cannot be true, for our conduct cannot vary from hour to hour or from day to day. We cannot sit up till past midnight and then say, "The holy day is past. We can do what we like today." Every single moment is a holy moment, and there can be no distinction.

Jesus recognized that. As a rabbi in the temple, he did not follow the rules regarding the Sabbath. He healed on the Sabbath and was rebuked for it and nearly driven from the temple. He made it very clear that we have the right to break the Sabbath, and he told us why: "The sabbath was made for man, and not man for the sabbath."[2] We are not to be bound by rules and regulations on any day, but we are to use our days to suit our purpose and not make our purpose suit a certain day.

In the Old Testament, there are dietetic laws. In the New Testament, we are told not to call anything unclean that God made. Through this, Peter had to learn the lesson that eating a certain kind of meat was not a sin as he had been taught.

The Hebrew Testament taught the importance of sacrifices, not only the sacrifice of living animals, but the sacrifice of money and property. The New Testament teaches, "In burnt offerings and sacrifices for sin thou hast had no pleasure."[3] There is not a God that is satisfied by our being in poverty, giving up our property, or living as ascetics.

Under the Hebrew teaching, circumcision was one of the most rigid of all laws; but Paul revealed that neither circumcision nor uncircumcision availeth anything.[4] That is all part of the law, but we are to come out from living under the law and live under Grace. In the Old Testament, baptism was an important rite. Of baptism the Master said, "Suffer it to be so now."[5] He never declared it to be a necessity.

Has the Hour Come for You?

In biblical times, unless a person made an annual trip to Jerusalem to deliver his gifts, sacrifices, and tithes, he could hardly hope to be forgiven his sins or to be considered a good Jew. There is a remnant of that left today in the Hebrew faith when on the Day of Atonement it is necessary, according to their teaching, to fast twenty-four hours, from sundown to sundown. Then every sin is forgiven, and a person begins at sundown with a completely new slate, with no punishments for anything of the past, completely free. Atonement is not quite that simple.

The temple was really the center of religious life for the Hebrew. No man was considered a religious man who did not make it so. It was not only that he had to attend temple on Saturday, but there were periods of prayer every morning of the week, and certainly Friday night, all day Saturday, and all the feast days and holy days. But Jesus Christ said, "The hour cometh, when ye shall neither in this mountain, nor yet at Jerusalem, worship the Father."[6] In one stroke, he freed his followers from an important part of the Hebraic law, the worship in the temple. What, no temple? For hundreds of years, men had slaved to build temples one after another. Men had devoted their lives to the building of temples and thought that they were building to the glory of God. And along came this man, a rabbi in the temple, who told them that they did not have to worship in that temple.

Does not all of this show to what degree man is still living under the law of the Old Testament, believing himself to have made the transition from the Hebrew faith to the Christian, while being just as rigidly bound by the Hebraic law as the ancient Hebrews were?

Freedom Is To Be Found Within

The Master undoubtedly gave us the greatest teaching that has ever been voiced by man in the Sermon on the Mount, which has come down to us in the Gospels through the disciples, in which Jesus points out what the Hebraic teaching is, and then explains what constitutes the Christ-teaching in his, "But I say unto you. . . ."

A student on the path who reads the Sermon on the Mount should pay particular attention to every passage beginning with "But I say unto you. . ."and see how many of those passages he has accepted and is living by. Then he will know to what degree he has failed to embrace Christianity and is still living as an ancient Hebrew. Having read that, there is no turning away again, until the transition has been made from ye-have-heard-it-said-of-old to living by but-I-say-unto-you.

It is not difficult to engender fear in the minds of those who are not instructed in spiritual truth, but it would be impossible to create fear in the consciousness of an individual correctly instructed in truth, because every mystic throughout all ages has revealed that all power is in the consciousness of the individual. It is not in any outside God or gods; power is not in the collective mind: the real power of the universe is in individual consciousness. This has been revealed in many ways, but the Master Christian has revealed it in very clear language: "The kingdom of God is within you."[7] The Father is within you: the Father is within me. While I of my own self can do nothing, nevertheless, the Father within me and the Father within you, He does the work.

So it is that every individual is one with Infinity. Every individual is one with infinite power, with eternal life, with immortality, and with the infinite abundance of the entire world, and of all the worlds beyond this world. The kingdom of God, the kingdom of Allness, the kingdom of that divine Government which rules the sun, the moon, and the stars, and the kingdom of that Government which governs man is within you. There are no exceptions to this rule, and the only reason that the world has not demonstrated complete freedom and infinite abundance is that it has not accepted the spiritual teachings of the masters of all time.

Ignorance of God, Our Greatest Blunder

The greatest blunder we have made is that we have looked to a God somewhere outside ourselves, mostly up in heaven. The basic error has been the belief that there is a God separate and apart from us to be worshiped in holy temples. God must be found within us, and then we must learn how to make contact with Him, how to bring the influence of God into our experience. We will not do it by asking for it, begging for it, pleading for it, sacrificing or tithing for it. What we sacrifice and what we tithe can be a tremendous blessing to us, but never in the way of bribery.

We have made another great blunder, too. We have believed that God can be influenced by man. How foolish to think of going to holy mountains, holy rivers, holy cities, holy temples, and of sacrificing or tithing to influence God! How foolish mankind has been in ignoring the wisdom that has been revealed so clearly and is so readily available!

Man cannot influence God by thought or deed, by sacrificing, by prayers, or by treatments. God is the infinite intelligence of this entire universe. How absurd to believe that we, with our finite knowledge, can influence God! God is the divine love that has brought forth all that exists. How ludicrous to try to tell God to be more loving than God already is or to give the impression that we ourselves are more loving than God, and that, therefore, we know what we would do if we were God, and so we proceed to tell God!

The Violation of the Law
Brings Its Own Penalty

The ancient Hebrews believed that they were worshiping God, when actually they were living under the Mosaic law and paying the penalty for the violation of that law. Not knowing that it was the law, they called it God, but it was the law: the law of the Ten Commandments, dietary laws, and laws of the synagogue. The violation of any of these laws brought penalties, just as today, if we violate the laws under which we live, eventually there must be a penalty.

It has been believed that it is possible to violate these laws and not pay the penalty for them, and so these laws are honored more in the breach today than in the keeping of them, but the fact that some may appear to escape the penalty for the violation of the law for a while does not change the fact that no one ever succeeds in violating the law forever.

It is not generally understood that these are not laws that some far-off God in some future time will punish us for violating, but rather that the punishment takes place within our own being by the very act of violation. In other words, we do not have to wait for a policeman to catch us or for God in the sky to catch us: the very act of violation brings the punishment.

The reason we do not accept that is that we go through this entire human life span with sins, disease, accidents, with droughts, with lack, with limitation, and with wars, and we say to ourselves, "And I did not do anything to deserve it." This is nonsense! All the iniquities that have been visited upon the nations of the world in these last centuries have been brought upon them by themselves by their violation of the Ten Commandments. Individually, as well as collectively, we have violated those Commandments, not necessarily all ten of them, but enough of them, and of course, taking the nations collectively, they have violated all of the Ten Commandments. Thereby they have brought upon themselves the wars, the depressions, the diseases, the sins, and the false appetites. These have all been brought upon them by their violation of the law.

It is true that in many individual cases our violations are not sufficient to warrant some of the horrors that have come upon us, but we must remember that we are living a collective life, and therefore, the sins of our society or the sins of our government come back upon our individual selves, just as the benefits or the profits of that collective living come back upon ourselves.

We Can Determine
What Our Experience Is To Be

It is necessary, before we can make spiritual progress, to understand that the kingdom of God is within us and that the issues of life are resolved within our own consciousness. Therefore, we cannot look to a God somewhere to set aside the violations that we commit, nor can we hope to escape those violations by ignoring them or by ignoring the Commandments.

Let me clarify that in this way. If the kingdom of God is within us, then the government of our life is within us, and it is to be settled within ourselves. Even though thousands may fall at the left and ten thousand at the right, it will not touch the individual who recognizes that the issues of good and evil take place within his own consciousness.

What goes on in this world has nothing to do with us. It is what goes on within our own consciousness. We receive the fruitage by abiding in the Word, or the withering and dying that comes from not abiding in the Word, because this law, which was the ancient law of the Hebrews, is repeated in the Christian faith. Never let us believe that by virtue of being Christians, we can in any way escape that law, because as part of our Christian heritage, Paul gave us the principle, "Whatsoever a man soweth, that shall he also reap."[8]

If we sow obedience to the laws of God and man, we reap richly; if we sow disobedience or ignorance of these laws, we must reap the withering and the dying. Paul continues, "He that soweth to his flesh shall of the flesh reap corruption; but he that soweth to the Spirit shall of the Spirit reap life everlasting."[9]

In the Hebrew heritage, the law is revealed through the Ten Commandments; in the Christian heritage, the same law is revealed in Paul's words, but the principle is the same. We can turn to the Oriental teachings and find that the mystics of the East have revealed that identical law as karmic law, which is nothing more nor less than the law of as-ye-sow-so-shall-ye-reap.

Recognizing this makes us realize our responsibility for determining the nature of the life that we will live. We are not considering the world at the present time: we are considering our individual demonstration. In the last analysis, it is our individual demonstration that is of utmost importance to us, because that is what we are going to pass on to our children, our grandchildren, and our great-grandchildren. As the world begins to see the fruitage of obedience, desiring that fruitage, it will fall into line. Therefore, to every individual to whom the spiritual truth is revealed, there comes an opportunity, a privilege, and a responsibility.

Are We Going To Live Under
God's Government or Under Human Law?

We know the penalty of living under this human ignorance
of spiritual values. In an inner quiet and darkness, we have the
opportunity of reviewing what we know of spiritual truth, so
the first responsibility is the ability to close our eyes and shut
out the world, turn within, and realize that here within us is the
determining factor of our life, not what our parents or grand-
parents did. They lived their lives; they benefitted or they paid
the penalty, whichever it may have been or both, but here within us, we have the power to bring forth a life under the government of God, or momentarily we have the choice of ignoring
that and continuing a haphazard human life. We are either
walking this earth, blind, foolish, accidentally, or we are recognizing that we are not here of our own volition.

Behind this world is the Creator,
the creative Principle, the infinite Wisdom and
divine Love that sent me into being. Behind this
universe is that which created the sun, the moon,
the stars, and above all, man. Behind this universe is
the divine Government that enables the tides to be
on time, the movement of the planets to be orderly,
the seasons to progress in their due order.

There is a divine Influence governing this universe,
and Its kingdom is within me. It has sent me forth
into expression. I am Its offspring.

The spirit of God which formed me in my mother's
womb is with me. This Spirit that created me has
always been within me, and It was within me upon
my entrance into this world. It has promised:

I will never leave thee, nor forsake thee. [10]
I in the midst of you am mighty. *I* in the midst
of you am greater than he that is in the world.
I will be with you unto the end of the world.
I will be with you if you mount up to heaven;
I will be with you if you make your bed temporarily
in hell; *I* will be with you if you
walk through the valley of the shadow of death. [11]
I, the Father within you,
will never leave you or forsake you.

Look unto Me, the presence of God within you, and
be saved. Look unto Me. Do not look up into the
sky, or into the sun, the moon, the stars, the planets,
but look unto Me, the Father within you. Then rest
and relax, for *I* am the infinite wisdom that formed
you in the womb; *I* am the divine love that maintains
and sustains you throughout all time.

Two Commandments Replace the Ten

The spirit of God has given us two laws which are far better than the ten, because we might obey the ten and leave out ten others, but if we obey these two, we will not only include the ten, but ten thousand others. "Thou shalt love the Lord thy God with all thy heart, and with all thy soul, and with all thy mind. . . . And the second is like unto it, Thou shalt love thy neighbor as thyself." [12] The violation of these two commandments brings about the withering and the dying; the violation of these two commandments is the boomerang that comes back upon us, bringing to us sin, disease, age, wars, rumors of wars, and fear of war.

How, then, shall we obey these two commandments? If we still think of God in terms of what we formerly believed God to be, there is no way to love Him. There is no way to love a God that punishes after first giving us the capacity to err. There is no way to love a God that consigns us to hell or damnation. There is no way to love a God that sets a flood on the earth to wipe out all His people. There is no way to love a God that is responsible for the death of our children. There is no way to love a God that is responsible for the accidents on the highway or in the air. So there is no way to obey that first commandment until we have pulled up this concept of God by the roots and dismissed it for all time.

To understand and to know God aright is to love God. It is easy to love God once we know God. When we discover what God is, who God is, where God is, and how God functions in our experience, we will find that we have entered a life of love. We will never be weary of loving God, but not until we have rooted out those false concepts of God, the false images of God, the God whom we ignorantly worship.

Let us for a while put aside our attempts to love the Lord our God, until we learn a little more about His nature, and let us see how we can love our neighbor. In discovering this love for our neighbor, we will be led right back to God's footstool, right back to the kingdom of God.

The Principle of Oneness Makes Love Possible

"Love thy neighbor as thyself." Love thy neighbor as if he were thyself. Here is the first mystery. Thy neighbor is thy self; thy neighbor is thine own self. The reason is this: there is only one life, and you and I are living that life. That life is one: it is your life, and it is my life, but before it was yours or mine, it was the life which is God. There is only one God; therefore, there can be only one life. The life I am living is God-life, and the life you are living is God-life. Therefore, the life of me is the life of you, the one life which is God.

There is only one intelligence of the universe, one intelligence that formed this entire universe, and universe upon universe. That intelligence is your wisdom and mine. There is only one source of intelligence—your intelligence and mine—and that emanates from God. God's wisdom is infinite, and scripture says "His understanding is infinite."[13] Therefore, you and I have no wisdom except that we have His.

There is only one soul, one source. There can be only one purity; there can be only one immortality, and that one is infinite. The soul which is God is the soul of individual man, and that means my soul and your soul; therefore, we have only this one soul in common. So my life is your life; my mind is your mind; my soul is your soul.

There is only one source: "The earth is the Lord's and the fulness thereof,"[14] and "Son. . . all that I have is thine."[15] My supply is your supply, and if I do not know that, I have lost the vision of supply. If I do not know that, I have lost the vision of life, of wisdom, and of purity.

God is my Self; God constitutes my being; God is the life, the mind, the soul, the spirit, and even my body is the temple of the living God. Could this be true of me and not of you? Heaven forbid! The world would be without a God if anyone, at any time, could ever say this of himself and not declare it to be universally true. Who could speak of the Father within him without remembering the Father within everyone else? So the same Father is within me that is within you. It is our good fortune that He is not a Hebrew Father or a Christian Father, but the Father, the spirit, the one life of all.

If I cannot love you exactly as I love myself, I am setting up two selves, and then I am outside the kingdom of God. Once I understand you to be my Self in another form, then my actions toward your Self must be those that I would have you perform toward my Self. Only in this oneness are we under the law of God; only in this way can the Ten Commandments be fulfilled.

They can be fulfilled only in the realization that what I do to another I do unto my Self.

Becoming Instruments of God

The great miracle of the spiritual life is that once we bring ourselves into obedience to the loving of our neighbor as ourselves, we automatically bring ourselves under the love of God. With that comes the miracle: a transition from the law to Grace. Let us be obedient to the law of love-thy-neighbor and love-thy-God, and we will make a transition in consciousness to where we are under Grace. From the moment of that transition, there is no longer a responsibility for or an activity of ourselves; there is no more your loving your neighbor or your loving your God: the whole movement is a movement of God through ourselves.

This is clearly revealed in the pamphlet, "Love and Gratitude," where it is made so evident that we ourselves cannot love because love is of God. We can only be the instruments through which the love of God pours through us to each other. Because of the centuries of our sense of separation from God, we are in a position now where we must consciously accept the law of loving our neighbor and of loving God. Then after we have brought ourselves under that law, we discover how quickly we move from the law into Grace; and under Grace, there does not seem to be a little I or a little you around to do the loving. It is all being done through us, and we can feel ourselves somewhat like a pane of glass, letting the light shine through.

It is a very strange thing that takes place with the transition from the law to Grace. The Master revealed it to us when he said, "Why callest thou me good?"[16]. He was good, we know that; he was more than good: he was perfect. But he says, "Why callest thou me good?" What he meant to convey was that he had passed that transitional stage from good humanhood to where his divinity took over, and there was no more a man to be good: there was only the Father within to flow through.

It was the same with healing. He always said, "I can of mine own self do nothing,"[17] knowing that humanly a person has no healing capacity, even if that person is Jesus Christ. But there is this Grace that flows through and performs that which is given a person to do, so that if someone says, "O Master, heal me," or "O Master, teach me," or "O Master, open my eyes," there is this divine Grace that flows through and does it.

The Transition from Law to Grace

Centuries before Abraham, Isaac, and Jacob, it was discovered that man leads a threefold life. There is the life he lives in his spiritual darkness when he is a combination of good and evil. With some degree of religious enlightenment, he makes the transition from being partly good and partly bad to where, to a great extent, he lives a humanly good life and he does not knowingly violate the Ten Commandments. This is the period of his existence which is the period of human good, and it is the function of most religious teachings to lead humanity from being partly good and partly bad to living humanly good lives.

However, there is a third stage, and this was also revealed back in the most ancient of days. It probably had its origin in India, where today we see so much of spiritual ignorance. There it was that spiritual wisdom first came to light on earth. That spiritual wisdom revealed that there is a moment in our human experience when we make this transition from being human to where the Divine takes over and leads and lives our life. In the teachings of the Orient, this state of consciousness is called Buddhahood, and it is recognized that anyone can attain Buddhahood, at least in some measure. Not all will attain the full degree of Gautama the Buddha, but in some measure all men and women may aspire to some degree of the Buddha-life, in which the spirit, the wisdom, and love of God take over and illumine that life.

In the Christian teaching, instead of the word Buddha, the word is the Christ. Both words mean Light, enlightenment, illumination. That illumination or Christhood is our goal. All men may not attain the full measure of Christhood shown forth by Jesus of Nazareth, but to all men and to all women it is ordained that some measure of Christhood will be revealed, and ultimately the full light and the full illumination.

Paul realized this at some phase and some day in his ministry, when he revealed, "I live; yet not I, but Christ liveth in me."[18] This is an actual experience that comes to many. Many on the earth in this very day and age have reached that stage where in some degree their soul, mind, and body have been taken over, and they can truthfully say, "I live, yet not wholly I. It is really the Father, the Christ, the spirit of God that lives in me. I of my own self can lay no claim to benevolence, to virtue, to charity, or to goodness. I must acknowledge that something happened one day, and the Spirit took over, the spirit of God in man, and It is fulfilling Itself in my life or my ministry." There are many today living this life in some measure, that is, having their lives lived for them by the Christ.

This is the state of consciousness referred to in that statement: "For the law was given by Moses"—and you must live in obedience to that law—"but grace and truth came by Jesus Christ." When this grace of the Christ touches you and you feel that your life is being lived by a Spirit within you, you can no longer love your neighbor or even love your God, but there is a love flowing through you which encompasses not only your affairs, but the affairs of those who come within range of your consciousness and, in some measure, even affects the entire world.

Live Love

Let us stop looking outside for either a God or some relative or friend to live our lives for us, and let us realize from this moment on:

> The kingdom of God is within me.
> The government of God is within me; and I can look
> within myself to receive God-government.

We have only one price to pay, and that is to be sure that we are loving our neighbor as ourselves to the highest of our present understanding. Nothing more is expected of us than our present understanding. Even if we have only enough understanding to love our neighbor to the extent of forgiving him, it will do for today. If our understanding permits us to share only a ten-cent piece with our neighbor or to be a little bit more cooperative, then that is all that is demanded of us today. But let us at least fulfill the loving of our neighbor as ourselves in the degree that we can understand it and demonstrate it this day.

> Let me look every day within myself
> for the realization that I have God's
> government within me, that "the earth is the Lord's,
> and the fulness thereof," and that all that the
> Father has is mine: mine for me, and mine to share,
> and twelve baskets full left over.

Let us live that much love, and let us then love God because we are no longer in fear of punishment, not on this earth and not after this earth. When we have come into obedience to the two commandments, there is no punishment coming to us for sins of the past on this earth or in any life to come, because there is no punishment in God, and here and now the sinner that sinned is no more, and the past is wiped out. The karmic law is nullified. Saul of Tarsus is now Paul; the woman taken in adultery is now Mary; and for all we know, the thief on the cross may now be another Christ on earth.

I am no more the person I was yesterday.
My identity has changed, even my name has
changed, and I know myself by another name:
Christ, the son of God. I have no more a human
inheritance, for I call no man on earth my father.
God in heaven is my Father; God within me is my
Father; the Spirit of this universe is my Father; and I
inherit my tendencies and my traits from my Father.

How long will I live? I will live as long as my
Father does, and He is still living, eternally,
immortally. God is eternal and immortal life,
and therefore my life is eternal.

This is the step that separates us from the animal man who
lives by self-preservation as the first law of his nature, and lives
under the law of as-ye-sow-so-shall-ye-reap. This is the first step
that leads us to say, "No, if necessary, I will lose my life, but not
take another's, and in the losing of my life I will find life eternal. If I take my neighbor's life, I have taken my own, for his life
is my life, and my life is his." In this awareness, we have taken
the first step toward that perfected humanhood, the step that
comes just a second before divine Grace takes over and says,
"Now you have no more life to live. Henceforth, I, God, I, the
Christ, live your life."

Because the spirit of God within is our life, we must bear in
mind that nothing from without can defile, maim, kill, or do
any destructive thing to us, because the grace of God and the
power of God are within us. Grace is not dependent on whether
we have been perfectly good or not perfectly good: It is there as
the gift of God unto all who turn to It, but not as a reward.
There are no powers outside of us that can defile or make a lie;
there are no powers outside of us that can be destructive to us,
for the kingdom of God is within us.

I in the midst of you am mighty. *I* in the midst of
you will never leave you or forsake you.

ACROSS THE DESK

Every principle of the Infinite Way which we make a part of
our consciousness through our meditation and practice takes us
that much closer to the goal of living in the fourth dimension.
Bit by bit, we find ourselves living as beholders, watching God
living Its life as us, while we stand a little to one side. The burden is lifted, and Grace is proving Its all-sufficiency. Is that not
a goal worth every effort?

Chapter Ten

"Call No Man Your Father
Upon the Earth"

To make the transition from mortality to immortality, from being the man of earth to being that man who has his being in Christ, requires an activity of consciousness. Nobody can make that spiritual transition from mortality to immortality for any person. Each one must make it in his consciousness by an awareness of his identity, that is, by understanding the nature of his being.

What Is Your Estimate of Yourself?

Do you believe that the spirit of God dwells in you? Do you believe there is an indwelling Christ in you? Do you believe that no man on earth is your father, that you have only one Father, God in heaven? Do you believe that you are the temple of God? Do you believe that you can do all things through Christ that dwells in you? Do you believe that *I* in the midst of you am mighty?

If you cannot answer these questions in the affirmative, you are the unillumined, the man of earth, who is not under the law of God. You will never be under the law of God until you can acknowledge that you have only one Father, a spiritual Creator, a creative Principle. Until you can acknowledge that, how can you be anything other than human, mortal, carnal? You can never rise any higher than your estimate of yourself.

What was the nature of the Master's teaching? Was he not revealing that this Father that indwells him, this Christ, is your Father? Was he not revealing that since he was the son of God, you, too, are the son of God? Is there any record in the New Testament that he set himself up as something other than you? "Greater works than these shall he do,"[1] even greater things. Do you accept his teaching that God is your Father, and therefore, that you are the temple of God? If you do, you now have a different estimate of yourself, and now you cannot do wrong.

What Makes for Purification and Spiritual Integrity?

Do you see the ridiculousness of trying to be good just because there are Ten Commandments? All you have to do is look at the history of the world to know that the Ten Commandments have not made or kept the world good. You might go further and look at the Sermon on the Mount. Has that made the world good? No, many persons are not only violating it, but even some ministers are saying that it is too impractical for this age.

There is only one way in which you can purify yourself so that sin becomes an impossibility for you. Once you know that you yourself are the temple of God, how can you violate yourself? Once you know that your body is the temple of God, how can you violate it? Once you know that all of us, individually as well as collectively, are the temple of God, how could you violate any other person? If you believe that your body and my body are the temple of God, how could you violate anybody's body? There is no other way of purifying yourself and maintaining your purity except to know that you are the temple of

God and that every individual under the canopy of heaven, whether he knows it or not, is also the temple of God. Knowing that, could you have within you the power to lie, cheat, or defraud?

There is no way of attaining spiritual integrity other than to know your true identity. Until then, people have the capacity to engage in any kind of deviltry. They can create wars, depressions, bankruptcies; they can violate anybody or anything, because they think they are doing it to a man or woman, and they think they are just a man or a woman doing it.

If you or I think or do anything of an erroneous nature, we know it, and very quickly we sit in judgment on ourselves, but then as rapidly as possible, we try to make amends or to see that the error is not repeated. This is true of everyone except for the wholly animalistic individual, and there are such on earth.

There are some persons so completely animalistic that they have no awareness at all of wrongdoing. It would make no difference if they pulled the whole world down around their shoulders, they would have no sense that they had done anything wrong. From their standpoint, anything someone claimed they did wrong would in their opinion probably be someone else's fault, and they were simply made to do it. There are those who could wreck a company, a bank, a home, or a nation, and not have the slightest twinge of conscience, because they have no sense of wrongdoing whatsoever. Such people are living wholly on the animal level of life, and nothing matters to them except "I", "me," and "mine." Self-preservation is all that counts with them. Somehow or other whatever evil they do is always the fault of the other person.

The Function of Conscience

The average person has what is called a conscience which prevents him from doing too much that is wrong, except under provocation. In most cases, it does not even permit him to do a slight wrong without knowing of it and trying to correct it. The reason for this is that in reality you and I are spiritual beings; we are the Christ; we are the son of God, the emanation of God; and we have in us the mind of Christ Jesus.

In describing this, Paul said, "For the good that I would I do not: but the evil which I would not, that I do. Now if I do that I would not, it is no more I that do it, but sin that dwelleth in me."² This is the truth about every one of us. We do not sin, nevertheless, a temptation arises here and there to think or do something erroneous, and sometimes we yield to it, and at other times we succeed in overcoming the temptation. We yield, not because we are evil, nor that there is any evil in us, but because having been born into this belief in two powers, this sense of sin operates in us: this sense of self, of materiality, and self-preservation.

And so even though we know better, we sometimes do what is wrong or think what is wrong, but not because there is a you that has a good side and a bad side. You are the Christ-Self; you are the child of God; you are perfection itself; and anything less than that is not you. That is why you can recognize it and want to overcome it; you want to lose sensuality and false appetites, because you, in your true identity, are that spiritual Son.

Evolving Students Set a Guard Over Their Lower Nature

The Christ is your Self, the illumined one, and you in your spiritual identity are that illumined Self. You do not get the mind that was in Christ Jesus: you have the mind that was in Christ Jesus. Nevertheless, alongside of that, there is this material or finite sense, and it is this that the Master overcame. He overcame this world, that is, the mortal sense of world in himself.

In Chinese mysticism, this principle is illustrated in another way. Lao-tze is shown sitting backwards on a horse, the horse representing the five physical senses. When a person is not in control, he had better sit facing forwards and have a good hold on the reins, but when he has attained mastery over the senses, he can sit backwards on the horse without even touching the reins, and the horse cannot run away with him. He is the master, and the horse knows it.

So it is that while you are evolving as students, you have to watch your lower nature; you have to hold the reins on it. You have to resist temptation; you have to remind yourself of the truth; you have to have Bible passages to hold you to the truth that there is a He within you. All this acts as a bridge to take you out of the material sense of life into the spiritual.

After you have come into the awareness of your Self as the Christ-mind, all that is gone. The battle is over; there are no more temptations: you are living as spiritual being, and you are seeing everyone else as spiritual being. Now you have no capacity but to do unto others as you would have them do unto you, because as far as you are concerned, you are the other. Anything that you would do to another for good or evil, you are doing unto yourself. Now you can dispense with your bridge because you are now there, on the other side.

Think for a moment what happens when you have the realization that Moses had: *"I am that I Am."*[3] I dare you to make that statement and do a wrong!

> *I Am. I* am the Son of God;
> *I* am the Christ. God is my Father, and yours.

You could not do a wrong, because knowing yourself to be the Christ, you would not violate your own integrity, and you could not violate anyone else's integrity, knowing the other person to be your Self.

The One Self

The teaching of the one Self is one of the greatest teachings of the Master:

> For I was an hungred, and ye gave me meat:
> I was thirsty, and ye gave me drink:
> I was a stranger, and ye took me in:
>
> Naked, and ye clothed me: I was sick, and ye visited
> me: I was in prison, and ye came unto me.
>
> Matthew 25:35,36

The disciples could not understand what the Master meant because Jesus was not in prison, he was not in a hospital, he was not in poverty, he was not naked, and he was not hungry. How could he say that he was all that and that they had helped him? His answer was: "'Inasmuch as ye have done it unto one of the least of these my brethren, ye have done it unto me,'⁴ because the least one is the Christ that I am, only you recognize It in me, but you do not recognize It in them, and now I am telling it to you."

He was trying to teach them that the Christ which he was is the Christ of their being, and it is the Christ of all the downtrodden people of the world. Do not forget it! They are the Christ coming to you for help, but not awakened to their Christhood. When you serve them, you are serving the Christ; and when you are not serving them, you are not serving the Christ.

Do you remember the story of the German shoemaker looking for the Christ, every day expecting the Christ to come to his door? It just seemed that It never did. One day a very poor person came there needing shoes, and the shoemaker, not thinking, of course, that this could possibly be the Christ, made a pair of shoes for him. The next day the beggar returned in the robe of the Christ and revealed his identity.

There are many stories like that of the beggar by the wayside. In Hawaii there is the story of Pele, who sometimes appears to travelers on the road as a poverty-stricken widow. Then, when someone gives her a lift, she reveals herself as the goddess. It all goes back to the Master's teaching: "Inasmuch as ye have done it unto the least of one of these my brethren, ye have done it unto me," for I am He.

There is no way to bring peace on earth by wanting human beings to be good to one another, because that is not in their nature. On the other hand, it is impossible for a person to be cruel to another when he knows his true identity.

If you say that I have the spirit of God dwelling in me, that I manifest the Christ, then I say to you: "You are right, the Christ does indeed indwell me, and the spirit of God dwells in me, but look around. This is a universal truth."

"God is no respecter of persons,"[5] and He has not put one person up on a platform to be spiritual while all the rest are human. If I show forth any evidence of spirituality, it is because I have recognized the Christ in myself. I could not violate It any more than you can, when you realize the Christ of yourself and more especially when you realize the Christ of everyone else.

Knowing Your True Identity Makes Your Presence a Blessing

Probably some of you know how Walt Whitman spent many of his days and nights during the Civil War, visiting Southern and Northern soldiers in hospitals in Washington, D.C. It was a period of his life when he had very little money, but the little that he had, he spent for writing paper, pencils, and postage stamps. He would sit at the bedside of the boys and let them dictate letters to their parents or friends which he wrote on stationery and with postage stamps that he bought.

In this way he served the Christ. It was the only way he had, and he did it with his body, his mind, and with the little bit of money that he had. He was a person who knew his identity and the identity of the soldiers he served, whether they were Southern or Northern soldiers. What difference can that make to a person who knows the Christ of his identity and the Christ-identity of other persons? "The place whereon thou standest is holy ground,"[6] not because it is selling for ten dollars a foot, but because God incarnate as your individual being is standing there. That is what makes it holy ground—not because somebody mumbo-jumboed a prayer over it, but because you are standing there.

To carry a blessing, to heal the sick, to comfort those who mourn, it is necessary to know your identity. As a human being, you cannot heal the sick; as a human being, you cannot comfort the mourner; as a human being, you cannot supply the poverty-stricken. But if the spirit of God dwells in you, you never have to say a word about spiritual truth or God: your very presence is a benediction. In fact, the less you say the better.

When Walt Whitman went to the bedside of those boys, he never told them the mystical truths that he knew: he just spoke to them about themselves and their families, and wrote letters for them. Very often doctors reported that men were raised up from the fear of death by his sitting there and writing those letters. Was that the reason? No! The reason was that he went there with love in his heart, and because God is love, he went with God in his heart, and his presence was the presence of God.

Anyone who goes anywhere with love goes with God, because God is love. Do you not see, then, that as long as there is love in your heart—not the personal kind of love that just picks out those it wants to be good to, but the love that is willing to share with the poor, the unhappy, the sick, or the mourner—you are carrying God in your heart; and therefore, your presence is a benediction to anybody and everybody. Without that love in your heart, you are barren; your presence is not a benediction or a blessing; and there is no blessing returning to you, because no blessing ever comes to anyone except the blessing he sends forth. It is the bread you cast upon the waters that comes back to you.

Only a Givingness of One's Self Gives Real Purpose to Life

So often the question is asked about our reason for living. Do you have a reason for living? Is there any reason for your remaining on earth? The answer must be, no, unless you are living impersonally as a benediction to the world. I do not mean being good to your family alone. A whole lifetime of devotion to your family does not merit half a golden star because you are not doing that unselfishly. Your family is part of your human self. You could starve yourself to death to send your whole family to college, and it would not gain you one merit. It is what you do impersonally, what you do unto another who has no call upon you, that is love. The other is selfishness, no matter by what name it is called.

There is no criticism, no judgment, and no condemnation because of this. The person who does not know his identity or who does not know the identity of everyone else cannot be expected to live unselfishly. It is only when you awaken to the fact that God has incarnated Himself as individual man that you will be sure that in addition to sending your child to college, you will help someone else's child go to college, or in addition to helping your fellow Americans, you will also help your fellow Chinese, Cubans, Hungarians, Indians, whoever it may be.

Do you not see, then, that as a human being you cannot be expected to think of anybody on earth but yourself and your family? The very moment, however, that you make the transition from being the man of earth to being that man who has his being in Christ, you do not care if you get crucified for your disciples or your students or anybody else, because you are now devoting your life to the Christ, whether the Christ appears as your own people or somebody else's people.

Paul, who was a Hebrew, gave his life that the Christian message might be carried to the Europeans, who were not Hebrews, to the pagans, and to the Greeks. He carried the word throughout southeastern Europe, not only to his own people, but to any people who would listen to him. Why? Because he had attained Christhood, and thereby knew that these others were also the Christ and should be awakened to an understanding and a knowledge of their true identity.

Do Not Violate the Robe

Do you not see that it has been the lack of an understanding of man's true identity that has been responsible for all the different sects in the world today? They are all convinced that they have the true God and that everybody else is in utter darkness, and so until recently they have drawn a circle and have left everybody else out. *This is why the Infinite Way must never be organized.* Ours is a recognition of true identity, that which has been revealed to me about my Self, which I also know to be your identity, even before you awaken to that knowledge. In fact, I am helping to awaken you to the knowledge and the experience of Christhood. I could not do it if you were not already the Christ. I could not make you what you are not. But I can awaken you to what you are and then watch you go out into the world, to the Jews, to the Protestants, to the Catholics, to the Vedantists, to the Zen Buddhists, and to all the rest. Look out at all of them and recognize that they are the temple of God, and that their body is the temple of God.

Look out upon this world and show your realization of this truth by your respect for every "you" that you meet, and everybody's body that you meet. You cannot violate anyone or anything when you know your true identity, because you cannot violate your Christhood.

Sometimes in mystical literature this is called "putting on the Robe" or "wearing the Robe." It means that when you have recognized your name and nature, you put on that white robe of Christhood. It is not a material robe: it is just a feeling you have of being draped in immortality and purity. Sometimes you hear about somebody who has put on that Robe, who has named himself the Christ, spiritual being, and then has violated it. He has thrown mud at his own white Robe. This is called "spiritual wickedness in high places,"[7] and while I believe that a human being can be forgiven any sin, because all sin is committed through ignorance, I do not like to see a person who has put on the Robe, who has recognized in some measure his Christhood, violate It. There are bound to be repercussions. Judas Iscariot paid the price. Many have paid the price of not acting in accordance with their acknowledged realization of Christhood.

Awakening to True Identity Is the Anointing

On this path of the Infinite Way, the revelation is given of your spiritual identity in truth—not as a mortal, not as a human being. The entire purport of this work is directed to awakening you to your identity so that mortality may be put off, that you may "die daily"[8] to the old man, and in a sudden burst of light, like Moses, say, "Oh, I am that *I Am*. I always was, but now I know it"; or like Saul of Tarsus who received the light and recognized his Christhood; or like Jesus when he said, "The Spirit of the Lord is upon me, because he hath anointed me."[9] This is the awakening, this is the recognition. When he spoke those words he was on the platform, at the altar of the Hebrew temple. Then he went down from there and out among the people. He was anointed because the spirit of the Lord God was upon him. It was upon him at birth; it is upon you at birth, but as

Jesus read those words he had that moment of knowing. That was the same moment for him as for Moses when he could say, *"I am that I Am,"* or for Saul of Tarsus when the Christ was revealed to him. Where was that Christ? Outside in the air? No, the Christ was indwelling.

The Master knew all the frailties of human beings, all the temptations. He was a man as we are, but knowing his identity and that of the people around him, he revealed to them that they might be as he was. He knew there was no use in preaching. There is no record that he said to the thief, "You ought to be a good man." Human beings do not have that power to be good. When they are, usually it is because the Ten Commandments frighten them into it, or a man-made law, a prison, a fine, or the fear of being caught. We can be really good; we can be truly moral, honest, sincere, and have integrity only when we know our identity to such an extent that we cannot violate it, even for that million dollars that someone else has that we think we need.

Knowledge of Your True Identity Brings Freedom

The only freedom there is, is a freedom that comes through the awareness of your identity. Do not believe that anyone can sign a paper giving you freedom. Official documents do not give freedom. Freedom can come only from within yourself when you have risen to the place where you cannot violate anybody's integrity or anybody's freedom, because you know that in imprisoning others you are imprisoning yourself; in holding others in bondage, you are holding yourself in bondage; in destroying another, you are destroying yourself. Only when you know this, do you lose the capacity to sin.

You are the temple of God; I am the temple of God. Try to violate yourself or another once you have grasped this point. And when you have grasped this point, what happens to sin? What happens to disease? Sin cannot exist in Christhood.

Disease cannot exist in Christhood; disease cannot exist in a heart of love; disease cannot exist in the temple of God. Until you know your true identity, however, you will be plagued with sin, disease, and lack. Do not ever think that the Christ can be poor. The Christ always has twelve baskets full left over, even after feeding the multitude. If you are the Christ, that is the measure of your riches. If you are "man, whose breath is in his nostrils,"[10] you save up your pennies for a rainy day because it always rains sometimes. Who do you say that you are?

A Knowledge of True Identity Brings a Life by Grace

Every great teaching of old had for its object leading the student up to a place of death, and Christianity, too, has for its aim the leading of every Christian up to the point of death, the death of personal sense to be followed by resurrection and ascension. This has been misinterpreted in the churches, however, to mean the death of the body and resurrection in a future life, which was not the meaning Jesus intended. The death takes place the day when you bury the old man that you were. The resurrection takes place the day when you know that it is the Christ being resurrected as you, in you. The ascension is the day when you rise completely above the belief of mortality, of two powers, above the belief of "man, whose breath is in his nostrils."

In our mortality, we are under the law. The reason is that as mortals we make our own rules, just as man makes his own God. Close your eyes for a moment and think of the God in which you have believed at some time or other, and may believe in even now. Think of that God and see what benefit you have ever received from Him. See if you cannot realize that all you have been doing is holding a mental image or concept in your mind, and then expecting that to be God. You have put yourself in bondage to that God. You have become absolutely convinced in your heart that this God punishes and rewards; and what happens? So is it unto you!

"To whom ye yield yourselves servants to obey, his servants ye are to whom ye obey."[11] If you render yourself a servant of that God who punishes and rewards, that is what you
are going to receive—not that there is such a God. You have
merely accepted that God from someone's teaching, and now
that you have put yourself under that God, you sit around
waiting for your rewards, which somehow do not come in this
world, and you wait for your punishments, and they seem to
come twice a day. But then you are more expectant of the punishment than you are of the rewards. Those are images you
have made in your mind.

You subject yourself to all kinds of man-made laws, but
when you remove yourself from man-made laws and bring
yourself under Grace, you then understand what the Master
meant when he said, "If any man will sue thee at the law, and
take away thy coat, let him have thy cloke also,"[12] meaning
that if someone takes your diamonds, give him your rubies,
too. In other words, "The earth is the Lord's, and the fulness
thereof,"[13] and it is yours by Grace. If someone is ignorant of
that and takes what belongs to you, do not fear, it will be
replaced because "the earth is the Lord's, and the fulness thereof," and it all belongs to you. Once you give up the protection
of man-made law, you come under Grace. Once you give up
the law of an-eye-for-an-eye and a-tooth-for-a-tooth, you
come under the Grace of forgiveness, but this comes only as a
transition in consciousness.

You are under the law as long as you are holding somebody
else to that law. When you bind another, you have bound yourself; when you free another, you have freed yourself. Consider
how many man-made laws you have accepted for yourself and
for others. Do not wonder that you are under the law and do
not think that you can come under Grace while holding somebody else in bondage to the law. You are under Grace when you

free all persons from being under the law, holding no one in bondage but acknowledging your Christhood and theirs.

A Life of Grace Has No Needs

"Call no man your father upon the earth: for one is your Father, which is in heaven."[14] God is your Father; therefore you are the Christ, the son of God. Tell me, what is there now to hold on to or to take from anyone else? Do you not see that only in the knowledge of your Christhood can you have the feeling that there is a Grace meeting all your needs and more? There is no way you can be free of desire except in the knowledge of your true identity. How can the Christ have a desire? The Christ is fulfillment. There is nothing out here that the Christ needs: the Christ is fulfillment.

If the spirit of the Lord God is upon you, you are ordained, and you need nothing. If you need nothing, you will desire nothing: you will be living in the Is-ness of being. You either live in Christhood or you live as a man seeking Christhood. If you must for a while live on the level of man seeking Christhood, so be it; but at least keep on seeking consistently until you attain the realization of your Christhood. If it is necessary, find someone, a Jesus, or anyone else whom you have known, historically or personally, and recognize his Christhood. This will lead you the next step to the Christhood of yourself, because anything that you can see as true of another, eventually you will see as the truth of yourself. You are that other, and that other is you, for there is only one Self.

I am thou; I am you; I am he. I am the Selfhood of
you; there is only One.

Here where I am, God is. In this moment,
I am fulfilled. My Self is the temple of God even as

my body is the temple of God.
Here where I stand is holy ground. I am fulfilled.

As I abide in that, that is what I externalize. In this awareness, there is no desire. If I keep on desiring, I will keep on
externalizing desires, and they will never be fulfilled: they will
just keep on being desires, because what I entertain in consciousness, I externalize. If I entertain desires, I externalize
desires. If I entertain the idea of fulfillment, then I externalize
fulfillment, for I am a law unto myself. There is no other law
out here acting upon me. I can either claim for myself my divine
sonship and manifest it, or I can claim for myself mortality and
manifest that.

The Choice Is To Sleep in Mortality or Awaken to Christhood

Jesus, dying on the cross, is not going to make you free. He
himself said: "Ye shall know the truth, and the truth shall make
you free."[15] He did not say, "I will know the truth and make you
free": he said, " 'Ye shall know the truth.[15]. . . Ye must be born
again'[16]—not I, but ye must be born again. I have died; I have
been resurrected; I am ascended; it is your turn."

All this is done as an activity of consciousness. You must
make the transition in consciousness yourself. You must
acknowledge the Christhood of your teacher, then turn within
and say, "If it is true of him, it is true of me. 'God is no respecter
of persons.' He merely woke up to his Christhood a day before
I did."

A person does not improve; he does not become more spiritual. He either sleeps on in mortality or awakens to his
Christhood. There is no progress: there is either being asleep or
being awake. Sometimes one person is sleeping more lightly
than others, and some are dead in sleep, but it is still a sleep

until the moment of awakening, and then sleep is over and the awakening has come.

"Call no man your father upon the earth." For thirty years this has been one of my great realizations in the healing work. I have been stuck and stuck hard with many cases, and usually the thing that saved me was when I could realize, " 'Call no man on earth your father,' then whoever is turning to me for help must be immortal." Knowing that set me free from my fears and doubts, and then the patient responded. "Call no man your father upon the earth." God is your Father; therefore, you are the son, and fortunately, God had all His children before they invented illegitimate ones, so God has no illegitimate children.

"Call no man your father upon the earth." See the miracle when you realize the spiritual nature of the creative Principle. See how you can drop these nonsensical beliefs of heredity. The belief of heredity binds many, not because it has power, but because the world accepts the universal belief about it, and in order to do that, it has to accept the belief that man is a creator. If you acknowledge, "Call no man your father upon the earth," then the only inheritance you have is a divine one, a spiritual inheritance, a perfect one.

"Ye shall know the truth, and the truth shall make you free." You have now been instructed in this truth; it has been imparted to you. Will you pick it up and live it?

ACROSS THE DESK

This month, the campaign for the November Presidential election in the United States is in full swing. As citizens, it is our duty to go to the polls in November to cast our ballot for our choice for the men for the highest offices in the land. Naturally, as any other good citizen, we accept the responsibility and obligation to be informed as to the qualifications of candidates for public office, but as Infinite Way students we must go beyond that in deciding how to vote by turning within for guidance in much the same way as did the disciples when they prayed, "Thou, Lord, which knowest the hearts of all men, show whether of these two thou hast chosen"[17]—not whom shall we choose. Into this prayer of complete surrender, no personal opinions can enter. We forget candidates and platforms, and realize the divine government. There is no better guide for this work than can be found in *Our Spiritual Resources,* page 160.

Are you accepting your privilege and duty as a citizen and as an Infinite Way student? If you are, then you need have no anxiety about who will be elected, but can rest secure in the knowledge that the government is upon God's shoulders.

Chapter Eleven

Teacher and Student
On the Path

It has been said that whatever a person keeps his mind fastened upon, that eventually he tends to become. What he desires, what he seeks, what he wants with all his heart and soul, he draws to himself. To a certain extent that is true on the human plane, but in the spiritual world, it is an absolute principle.

It is true that desire is prayer. That does not mean, however, desire for a home, desire for health, or desire for an automobile: it means a desire for God, a desire for truth, for spiritual realization, a desire that the hunger of the heart be satisfied. Spiritual desire is really a deep form of prayer: it is to hunger and thirst after God.

Find Your Path

Each one must determine the message that is right for him and who his teacher is. Do not think for a moment that everyone is going to derive the same measure of benefit from any and every teaching or teacher. There are some persons who respond naturally to the mystical teaching of the Infinite Way. That then becomes their path, and once they determine that this is their way, it is up to them to give it the utmost devotion that they have.

For others, this may not be their path. That is why I am happy that in the Infinite Way we have never been led to form any kind of an organization; I do not want anybody held to this Way by membership. Everybody must feel free. If this message is not for you, keep on searching and seeking until you find the one that is. Do not think because somebody you know has had a beautiful healing in the Infinite Way or has benefitted from it that it necessarily means it is for you.

Each one must have his teaching and his teacher, something to which he responds. Until he finds it, he must continue to search. When he finds it, something within him says, "This is my way." After that, he abandons all others and gives himself wholeheartedly to the one. As he continues to do this, he discovers that something from the beginning has been building up in him to the point where the Saul of Tarsus in him dies, and the St. Paul is born.

The moment a spiritual stirring takes place within a person, a stirring to know God, to know Truth or Reality—any name you wish to give It—the very moment that stirs in him, it sets up a spiritual vibration. When it does, it finds a response in a teacher somewhere on the globe. The person searching may not know the identity or the location of the teacher, but in due time a set of circumstances shapes itself, and he finds himself in the presence of that teacher in whom this vibration has been set up or with whom he has tuned in.

The teacher responds. He responds in the same way that a parent responds to the love of a child. Let a child reach out with a tiny bit of love, and the parent responds with a great big armful of love. And so, let the student reach out with some tiny measure of spiritual longing, and he will find a teacher pouring out the fullness of his capacity for spiritual love and spiritual truth.

The Spiritual Teacher Recognizes Those of His Household

In all spiritual work, spiritual teachers are attuned to certain pitches or vibrations, and they do not respond to anything but those particular tones. If you held up wealth to a spiritual teacher, the spiritual teacher would not flick an eyelash in that direction. He just would not respond to it. You may hold up fame, and you will find that he does not even know that you are passing by.

You can no more fool the spiritual teacher than you can fool God. There is no use praying to God with promises of devotion, if it is not a full and complete free offering of oneself. There is no way to fool the divine Principle of life. It is all-knowing, all-seeing, all-discerning.

So, too, spiritual teachers are not fooled by students for very long. Sometimes, for a short time, someone seems to hoodwink a teacher by giving the appearance of wanting God. But it does not take too long for a teacher of discernment to see right through the facade. On the other hand, the teacher can often discern in the student qualities that the student does not know he possesses, longings that have not yet come fully to light and a depth of receptivity that he is not yet aware of in himself. This all comes to the teacher, as it will ultimately come to the student, by the power of that developing consciousness, the enriching of consciousness with qualities that are beyond the human.

It is a strange thing sometimes to see this discernment at work, not that it can ever be explained. For example, one day a list of names was misplaced, that is, it seemed that it was misplaced. I began searching for it but could not find it. Then I stood still for a minute and, quick as a flash, I picked up a book off the desk, opened it, and there in the back of the book was the list. You can explain that in any way that you like, but the fact remains that while I was looking for it humanly I did not find it. When I stopped for a second, whatever it is that is All-knowing led me right to the place where it was.

It is in that same way that students are led to teachers or to teachings. They are led to the very book and often to the very page on which is the passage they must have, and all that without any human knowledge of what it is they need, or what it is they are seeking or where it is. This might be called an intuitive or spiritual faculty. The name is not important. The important thing is how one attains it. The only answer to that question is for a person to be sure within himself that he really and truly is seeking God-awareness. No one who is seeking God-awareness is ever going to be disappointed. Where disappointment and frustration come in is in seeking God for a purpose. No one can seek God for a purpose. God must be the only purpose.

The day comes when a person realizes, "I never will be satisfied with all the health there is in the world or all the wealth, if I do not have that other Thing called God, if I do not attain that realization, that feeling of the Presence, that awareness." That comes to many, many persons. Then they realize, also, that for some the attempt to find God for a purpose has resulted in failure; for others, it resulted in success, but only that it might lead them to the realization of the great truth that after they have what they thought they wanted, they discover it is not what they wanted after all. There is something beyond.

What counts is the degree in which God is the goal, the degree in which the student purifies himself and makes God his true goal, that is, really purifies himself of the belief that in attaining God he is thereby going to attain some other goal. In the degree that he can overcome such tendencies in order to be spiritually pure within, in that degree will he find *the* teacher who can lead him to that particular attainment.

We Draw to Us Our Own State of Consciousness

There is a teacher for those who seek. The only way of finding that teacher is by attaining the same measure of inner purity and integrity as the teacher, because then you will have set up in you the vibration that finds an answer in the teacher. Your rate of vibration will bring to you the teacher whose vibration is of the same quality as yours.

You are drawing to yourself out of this world your own. Your own will come to you. In some ways that is a horrible thought, because it means that whatever the quality of your state of consciousness, that is what you are drawing to yourself. It is necessary to be sure that there is an inner integrity. That is why I caution students to watch themselves very carefully and closely, not so much at the beginning of their study as when they begin to feel that they are beginning to understand and to see the fruitage and are probably resting on cloud two or three. There is where the danger comes in.

Temptations on the Way

Until one is seasoned in the Spirit, there are temptations on the spiritual path, and this is symbolized in scripture by the Master's three temptations in the wilderness.[1] If you study that carefully, you might be quite surprised to learn that Jesus who was already a Master and spiritually ordained should be called upon to go through three temptations of the nature of those that he had to go through in the wilderness. You would have thought that he was immune to the lure of power, fame, or of wanting to use thought in order to turn stones into bread. You would have thought that at that stage he was already perfect. But that could not have been, because a perfected soul could not possibly have been tempted.

There are severe temptations to which students are subjected on this path. There are many students who, just about the time that they think they are progressing spiritually, may find themselves going through their deepest trials in the form of lack. The temptation is to believe that God has deserted them or that they have become unworthy of God. If that condition of lack lasts a little bit too long, they get discouraged and give up.

To others, the early flush of realization of the Spirit brings prosperity, and they find that prosperity is something they cannot take, because it becomes something in and of itself: the things that it can do for them, buy for them, or give them. Thought is deflected from the truth that it is not the form of wealth that is wealth, but the Source.

At every step there are temptations. Peter was tempted to preserve his life; he was going to preserve his safety; and thereby he lost much. The fact that the Master forgave him was not an evidence of Peter's attainment but of the Master's. That such a thing could have happened to him after three years with the Master must have been hard for Peter to understand.

When students have attained spiritual consciousness, they are not concerned about their human sense of life, their human sense of supply, or their human sense of freedom. Some of those on the path have been cast into lions' dens, some burned, some crucified, and some thrown into prison. That made no difference to the illumined, for that which constitutes illumination is the realization of immortality. They care but little if immortality is on this side or that side.

A One-Pointed Goal Carries Us Through Every Temptation

Let no one overestimate the degree of his spiritual progress until he has been tested. But when he is tested, let him not fear the consequences, for there are no consequences, except the joyous consequences of overcoming: overcoming fear, overcoming the concept of self-preservation, overcoming whatever it is in human nature that keeps a person from the full and complete realization of his spiritual identity.

One realization, if carried with you, will suffice to take you through temptations of any and every nature. That realization is that your goal is God-realization and that you have no intention of stopping until that is attained, be the price whatever it may be. God-realization is your goal.

Should lack come into your experience, you will realize that this can never separate or deflect you from your goal, that it never can be a power in your experience. You have set your feet on this path and you will not look back. If you have to go forward with lack and limitation as a companion for a while, perhaps it will teach you important lessons.

If prosperity comes to you, you will be doubly watchful. It is so much easier to be virtuous when poor. You will realize that wealth does carry with it a temptation to interfere with your search for God. It provides opportunities for distracting your attention from your goal to what the world calls the peace that it can give, the joys and the pleasures that the world can give. This can set up temptations far greater than lack can. And so the greater the prosperity, the greater must be the constant realization: God is my goal, and this success and prosperity will not move me or take me from my path, or take from me the golden hours or minutes that I need for meditation, reading, study, and for the companionship of those who are on this path.

Many who have entered spiritual work have been spoiled by their success, sometimes by the numbers who come to them. Numbers do not count in spiritual work. Whether a dozen, a thousand, or two hundred come, it should make no difference to the person in a spiritual ministry. That person is maintaining his conscious union with God, trying to be an instrument through which God expresses, and it makes no difference whether there are two persons to receive it, one person, or ten thousand.

Your consciousness determines your demonstration. No demonstration rises higher than the consciousness from which it emanates. Therefore in proportion as your consciousness maintains its integrity and keeps as its goal God-realization,

God-demonstration, God-vision, God-being, in that proportion do you draw unto yourself your own.

The Relationship Between Student and Teacher

Just as you learn in life never to blame anyone for your misfortunes, regardless of how much someone humanly may seem to be at fault, so do you learn that you can draw unto yourself only that which is already established in your consciousness. The bread that you cast on the water is the bread that will return to you, and if the bread that you are casting on the water is God-hunger, the true bread of life will come back to you.

You, yourself, are responsible as to what degree of good you receive from a teacher, from a teaching, or even from a book. What degree of spiritual integrity do you bring to these? That is the degree that you will draw out from them. A book by itself is just so much black ink on so many white pages, and that is all you can get from a page, unless you, yourself, bring something else to that page. When you bring your God-hunger, you draw from it God-satisfaction, the bread of life, the meat, the wine, and the water of Spirit. When you bring your heart filled only with spiritual desire to a teacher, you draw through the teacher the bread of life, the wine, the water, the staff, the substance. That is *your* demonstration.

The object of this work is not to find a master who is going to live your life for you, but rather to find the Master within which is your own developed consciousness and which then lives your life for you, so that you do not believe that Jesus or any other man is responsible for the safety, security, abundant health or joy, but rather that the Christ is the substance, activity, and law of your life. Christ is your attained state of spiritual consciousness.

After a student has been taught how to make direct contact with God through meditation, he may wonder if there is not something debilitating in continuing the relationship of teacher and student. Such a thing would be impossible, unless you can imagine its being debilitating to remain with Christ Jesus, Buddha, Lao-tze, or any other real spiritual teacher. Heaven forbid! A spiritual teacher—I am emphasizing *spiritual* teacher—has no ties to his student, absolutely no human ties. The teacher's only obligation is to live up to his own spiritual integrity. He owes no man anything but to love him, and the only way he can love him is by maintaining his spiritual integrity and not violating it. So a teacher owes nothing to anyone but himself, and what he owes is the maintaining of his own conscious oneness with God.

A student, too, owes it to himself to live up to his highest sense of spiritual integrity. If the student maintains that integrity, he will call on the teacher only for his spiritual welfare. In a work like ours, that may include spiritual healing of mind, body, or purse. That is legitimate, because it is all a part of spiritual unfoldment, but a student would never burden the teacher with his personal cares, worries, or woes, except in presenting them to him for the purpose of having help. Certainly the teacher would not burden a student with his problems, if he should have any. So you see that there is no relationship between a student and a spiritual teacher that could weary, weaken, or debilitate the student; there is no relationship of dependence. The relationship is one of assistance, but in no case dependence. The teacher does not owe any monetary support to the student, and the student does not owe any monetary support to the teacher, although the student will certainly want to express gratitude in tangible form. But obligation there is none in either direction.

The bond between a spiritual teacher and a spiritual student is a bond of divine love, not human love. That cannot ever be debilitating; it cannot ever be weakening; it cannot ever make a person a leaner, because no spiritual teacher permits that. My help to the student carries him only so far, and he is never permitted to feel that he need do nothing but rather let me do it. I am not that kind of teacher. I am more like the birds that push their little ones out of the nest and say, "Fly out of here or fall! Stand or fall on your own inner integrity." To me that represents teaching the way it has been given to me on the inner plane.

Everything that takes place in the Infinite Way is an instruction given to me from within. None of it has ever represented my will; none of it has ever represented my desire. All of it represents the way I am shown. It does not demand that with every other word you utter it is necessary to add, "Joel said this"; it does not demand that you tell everybody how much you love Joel; it does not demand anything of you except your own personal integrity. That is all. Any spiritual teacher who is under the guidance of the Spirit would tell you the same thing. If at any time students become overly dependent on a teacher, it may be that the teacher has not noticed it, and then, if they become weak through that leaning and dependence, they have themselves to blame. Each one is an individual. In free countries, everyone has the schooling that enables him to be a thinker, everyone has the capacity to think for himself, and he does not have to be misled.

The Teacher-Consciousness

The one who has attained the teacher or practitioner state of consciousness has the capacity to look a person in the eye and see the spiritual son of God and not believe the evidence of the senses, not believe the appearance, whether it testifies to sin, disease, lack, or limitation. This is the spiritual teacher and healer, not the one who prays to God that a person be healed. The spiritual teacher or healer is one who can look directly at a person with this realization: "I know thee who thou art. Thou art the Holy One of Israel." And then to this appearance of sin, disease, false appetite, or lack respond, "Aha! That is the mirage, the illusion. That is what would fool me into trying to do something."

The teacher has attained the ability to recognize the illusory nature of what is presented to him as a problem. He has attained an awareness of spiritual principles and through constantly living with them, studying them, and putting them into practice, his consciousness has evolved to that place where, when he is faced with an appearance, he can say, "Illusion," and turn away from it.

Infinite Way teachers and practitioners must develop the consciousness within themselves that knows they are not trying to improve a person's humanhood. They are not trying to reduce a fever; they are not trying to remove germs; they are not trying to provide patients with better employment or happier households. The Infinite Way teacher and practitioner must have as the goal the realization of the Christ, the realization of spiritual identity.

A truly spiritual teacher does not enter into any criticism or judgment of students who come for help, knowing that whatever degree of error is manifest in them is only there through ignorance and that it may take many years to dispel that ignorance. With some, it is a long drawn out process. With some few, it is rather quick, all depending on previous preparation in other incarnations. Therefore, the teacher must very often be patient with those who come to him. Certainly he must forgive seventy times seven, must not criticize, judge, or condemn the students' faults, but rather recognize the source as the carnal mind. If a student wants to withdraw from him, he has that privilege, but then when he wishes to return, he has that privilege, too, because no teacher of real integrity could or would cast out anyone.

The teacher allows those to go who wish to go; he permits them to return when they wish to return. There are some who come refusing to accept what the teacher has, and sometimes he must tell those to go because he has nothing for them. He cannot compel them to do anything; therefore, when they cannot accept the teacher's instructions, the best thing for them to do is to be about their own way because they may find their solution with some other teacher or teaching.

You will remember how on the platform of the Hebrew synagogue, the Master read from Isaiah, "The Spirit of the Lord is upon me, because he hath anointed me to preach the gospel to the poor; he hath sent me to heal the brokenhearted, to preach deliverance to the captives, and recovering of sight to the blind, to set at liberty them that are bruised. . . . And he began to say unto them, This day is this scripture fulfilled in your ears."[2] This is what constitutes a spiritual teacher. A spiritual teacher may be a student of metaphysics, a student of oriental philosophy, a student of any kind of spiritual teaching, but eventually there comes a day of ordination, when something takes place within the consciousness of that student, and he is changed: he is entrusted with a mission or a message.

The Teacher Sets Every Student Free

In my experience, I have never known a student to cling to me or depend on me in any way. Probably the reason is that I have always set every student free. I seldom refer to anyone as *my* student, because I do not really feel that anyone is my student beyond the time he wants to be so classified. The student may want to change his mind tomorrow and wander off and, if he does, he is welcome to do so. I hold no one, *and no real spiritual teacher would ever hold anyone.*

Even in the metaphysical practice as I knew it formerly, never did I refer to anyone as *my* patient, *a* patient perhaps, but not *my* patient, nor did I look on anyone who came to me as a permanent patient. Patients came to me for help, and I gave it, but they were free tomorrow to go anywhere they chose, and without reporting to me, if they so desired. I have never had a tie of any nature on a patient or on a student.

Regardless of how high the student goes with me, and we have some who are right on top of the inner circle, they still are under no obligation to remain, certainly under no obligation to support me. My conscious contact with God has done that abundantly.

So it is that student and teacher are free. The teacher is free to travel the world and not feel that he has to stay in any one place for any person or group of persons. In a relationship of that kind, a great love develops between the teacher and student, a real love and friendship. The bond is a spiritual one, but each one is free.

What Do You Give to the Teacher Who Gives a Lifetime of Dedication?

When you find your teacher, be assured of this: he is giving you his dedicated life. He is not giving you a little portion of it: he is giving you every bit of it. Then the question is: What do you give back? A spiritual teacher does not ask you for money; he does not ask you for praise. But what do you give back? Do you realize that a spiritual teacher is pouring himself out, that he has devoted ten, twenty, or thirty years of his life to attaining his practitioner or teacher state of consciousness and that with every meditation he is giving you the benefit of that ten, twenty, or thirty years? Are you looking on it in that light or are you just thinking, "Oh, well, she prayed for me"; or "He prayed for me"? Are you realizing that it is the full Word that is being spoken every time you reach out to any dedicated worker in the spiritual field?

There are dedicated workers in every one of the metaphysical movements, organized or unorganized. They may not all be that, but many of them are. If you have been led to one of the dedicated ones, be assured that he is giving you the fruitage of his dedication. The question is: Are you seeing it in that light, or are you thinking of it as just another meditation someone had for you? Very often your estimate of the nature of a prayer, treatment, or meditation, or your estimate of the dedicated life that is giving itself to you determines your reaction to the work. If you are rightly evaluating it, it has value to you; if you are not rightly evaluating it, it has no value to you.

As a teacher, I withhold nothing. Whatever is put into my mouth is imparted; it is not made up; it is not rehearsed: it is the word of God as it is revealed, not revealed a year ago, but revealed in that moment of impartation. In a class situation I am the teacher, and those who come are my students. Once the class is completed, there is no communication from me unless it first comes from the student, but if it comes from him, my answer is sent to him promptly. The relationship between us is always voluntary; the relationship between us is spiritual; the relationship between us is such that I respect the student so deeply that I would never knowingly lie to him or withhold from him, and that is all I expect of him. There is no other obligation between us except to love one another.

The Meaning of Loyalty

Loyalty to a teacher means only love and respect for the one who is imparting to the student the secrets of life. You could not possibly receive the "pearl of great price"[3] without having respect, honor, gratitude, and love for the one who has shared so unselfishly with you what you could find in no other way. You cannot find the pearl in a book, in holy mountains or temples. The secret of life has to come to you from an individual to whom it has been entrusted. Those on the spiritual path come up through their years of study, discipleship, and living in the Spirit until on a certain day they are entrusted with the Word, the

Message, the Principle, and given the ordination of teaching.

All students are not loyal; all do not remain with a teacher or on the path; all are not true. There are many Lot's wives who go a certain distance from the old city and then turn around and look back and decide that human enjoyment is more important than the narrow path of spiritual unfoldment. There are many who, with some measure of enlightenment, find their ego inflated. They seem to become important under it, instead of humble, and eventually they drift away. All who come do not remain, but all who come, as long as they come, receive what is given to me to give them.

Jesus lived with his disciples for three years, and look what happened to Judas! Look what happened to the other eleven! You would not be proud to have most of those for students or disciples. Most of them were not worth the time he gave them. What did they do? Deny him, walk away from him, protect their own lives, sleep. For three years he gave them all he had, but they just could not accept it. They were blinded by some bit of personal sense.

The Function of Spiritual Teachers

The purpose of a spiritual teacher is to help those who desire that the Son of God be raised up in them, to assist them to attain this end—never to make them worship their teacher or depend on him, but to come to the teacher that he may help them lift up that Son of God and set them free, so that they, too, may be able to say, "I have overcome the world.[4] . . . I and my Father are one."[5] But this will not come if the student does not change his concept of God and the Christ, and eliminate from his consciousness any belief that God or Christ is a temporal power.

When you touch the consciousness of an individual who has received spiritual Grace, you are touching the full Christ-consciousness. You are not touching the limited sense of consciousness of an individual: you are touching the full Christ-consciousness. Christ-consciousness cannot be divided. A spiritually ordained teacher cannot have a part of Christ-consciousness. He either has Christ-consciousness or he does not have It. Of course, it is true that individuals might have Christ-consciousness and not be fully aware of the pearl that they have. That does not change the fact that they have It. But when anyone touches the consciousness of an individual who has received his spiritual light, he is touching the fullness of the Christ-consciousness.

The truth you are seeking of God, you are receiving from God. The teacher may be an instrument through which you are receiving it from God at this moment, but the teacher is not necessary to your demonstration. Only the *I* of your being is necessary and as long as you look to It, It will raise up seed. If you look to a person, you may lack, but if you are looking to the *I* of your own being, then it may come to you through a spiritual teacher or some other being, but it will really be the *I* of your own being that has raised it up.

You attract to yourself your teacher and your teaching, just as the teacher and the teaching attract you to them. I draw to me those of my own household. No man can take those away from me. Any person who would try to interfere with that would have an experience such as Ananias and Sapphira had. Let no one try to take from anyone those whom God has given him for they are not fighting man: they are fighting God. They come off second best each time, and second best is not very good.

That which God gives you no man can take from you. That which you get by human argument, human conniving, human cleverness, human strength, or human wisdom, you may lose. You will never lose what is given to you by God. As soon as anyone reaches out his finger to touch it, he will be burned. You can be thankful and grateful to every individual who is an instrument through which God's grace reaches you, but these individuals are not the source of your good. God, which is the *I* that you are, is the source.

Truth comes to you from the *I* of your own being. If you always look to It, It will raise up for you your teacher or your teaching as long as that is needed. You can be thankful to them and you can be grateful to them, but do not confuse the issue and think that they are your God or your truth. They are but the instruments which your own consciousness has raised up for you.

The function of a teacher on this plane is to lift the consciousness of an individual to that place where he can make contact with the Father within. Part of the function of the teacher is to instruct in the correct letter of truth, but that is the least of the obligations of a teacher. The major function of a teacher is to live so high in consciousness that he is enabled to lift up those who come to him and lift them high enough so that they may have access to the kingdom of God within their own being, an access which they could not have through their mind, through the intellect, through taking thought. You have access to the kingdom of God only as you are lifted into the realm which is above mind, above thinking, above the intellect. And it is only those who have gone a step beyond you who can lift you to that place.

ACROSS THE DESK

Thanksgiving is one of the most joyous holidays in the whole year. This day, set aside as a day for the giving of thanks, becomes increasingly meaningful to us as each day of the year our whole attitude is one of gratitude for the omnipresent grace of God.

To have a greater awareness of the place of thanksgiving in the spiritual life, take a concordance to the Bible and look up all the passages you can find on thanksgiving and praise, and then contemplate them. As you fulfill the biblical injunctions in regard to praise and thanksgiving, truly you will be a witness to all God's wondrous works. Happy Thanksgiving!

Chapter Twelve

Spiritual Illumination

The path of discipleship takes us through the steps of that first awakening to the spiritual anointing which leads to that final goal of conscious union with God. While the letter of truth is of tremendous help, such an important help that I have not yet discovered a way of dispensing with it, nevertheless, it is only an aid to lead us into meditation, where the real transition takes place. We might know all the truth there is from here to Jerusalem and back again, but if we do not attain the realization of our real Self, knowing the truth is going to play but a small part in our life. We must eventually reach the realization of the real Self—my real Self, your real Self, and his real Self—until there is only one real Self. This is brought about through meditation.

It is in meditation that we make that final contact with the spiritual Source of existence that enables us to know the truth, not intellectually, but through realization.

The *I* that I am is the Christ-Self. It is not only the Self of me: It is the Self of you. It is not an individual Self that I alone have: It is a universal Self. It is *I*, myself, and is also *I*, you.

When I make contact with this *I*, I have made contact not only with the universal Self which I am, but I have also made contact with you: not with your humanhood, but with your spiritual identity.

The Master said, "Henceforth I call you not servants. . . but I have called you friends."¹ The moment I recognize that this Christ-Self of me is the Christ-Self of you, we are equal, and that is the only equality there is. There is no such thing as an equality of social status: there are the socially up and the socially down, the socially somebody and the socially nobody. There is no such thing even as an equality of political status, as anyone who belongs to a political party finds out, nor is there an equality of economic status: there are the poor, the rich, and the in-between; there are the commercially up and the commercially down. No, there is no such thing as equality in human life, and there never can be.

The only equality is a spiritual equality, and that equality is because my Self is your Self and your Self is my Self: there is only one Self. That is why we are equal. We each may still live on different economic levels of life; we may still have our different political and social levels. There is no equality to be found in these, and let us not look for it. Spiritually, even the least person on the social, the economic, or the political rung of the ladder is my equal, and even the greatest of these is only equal with me. Why? Because there is but one Self, and It is divine.

Assuming Dominion by Turning Away From Temptation

Because we have realized our true Self, when the "natural man"² of us wants to express himself in some form or other, we can say, " 'Get thee behind me, Satan'³; I am not interested in you." This temptation may appear as fear, but we can turn on it with, "What is the use of fearing when I am eternal? Neither life nor death can separate me from God." That should eliminate the fear, and because of our recognition of our true identity, our real Self, no matter what temptation would come, no matter what amount of the natural man is left, we can always turn on it with a "Get thee behind me."

In everyone there is some of that natural man left; no one has ever attained full Christhood while on earth. Even the Master said to the disciples, "Could ye not watch with me one hour?"[4] There is enough of that natural man in all of us to want to keep the *status quo.* However, in proportion as we realize that Christ is our true identity, when the natural man wants to rise up in sin, sickness, lack, or with any other claim, we can turn on it, "There is no reality to you; I know who I am. I am the son of God, heir of God, joint-heir." Holding ourselves in that consciousness of our true identity, the natural man recedes.

The deeper we go in the awareness of the truth that the Christ-nature is our true nature, that Christ-consciousness is our true consciousness, that the Christ-life is our true life, that divine sonship is our real being, in the degree that we know that about ourselves and are willing to acknowledge it about others, in that degree, then, the natural man of us has less play in our life, less influence, and less occasion to vaunt itself. It may rise up with temptations, and does, but always within us there is this remembrance of our true identity.

Christhood Is Not To Be Attained But Recognized

In all religious literature, more especially the mystical, the goal of the awareness of our true identity is set forth. The Greeks said, "Man, know thyself," in other words, "Man, come to know your true identity." The Master, also, revealed to us our true identity and showed us that the carnal man, the natural man, is not of God and must be put off.

Paul, too, told us to "put off the old man. . . and put on the new man,[5] . . . that mortality might be swallowed up of life,"[6] showing us the lower self, the natural man, and the higher Self, the Christ, which we are. "But whom say ye that I am?"[7] Unless we can say, "Christ," we have not attained enough spiritual awareness to discern the Christ of individual being. Even if a person does not know his Christ-identity, it is our responsibility to recognize it, and if we do not, then, in that degree we are not living out from spiritual consciousness.

Good is not really a quality that you are going to attain: good is the being that you are. The Christ is not something you are going to attain: the Christ is the being that you are. It is something which you must now recognize. You are to realize that Christ is now your true identity: you do not gain it. There is no you to gain something: there is the you which already is, but which must now be realized.

If you understand Christ as your identity, that is letting Christ abide in you, not really *in* you, but *as* you. If you will let Christ live as you and if you will live as Christ, then when your lower self, the carnal man, the natural man, rises up to say, "I do not feel well. I am sick"; or, "I am poor"; or, "I am tempted"; or, "I am sinning," you will respond with "'Get thee behind me, Satan.' I know who I am." Gradually you will find it becomes easier and easier, not only to attain life as the child of God, but also, what is so very important, to live with your neighbors, knowing their true identity, and the true identity of those who have not even begun to suspect it.

The Christ does not have to earn Its living by the sweat of the brow; the Christ does not have to struggle or strive: the Christ lives by Grace. That is what happens in the moment that you recognize your true identity and mine. It must be universal. The moment you realize that you are living, not as a mortal, but as Christ-being, in the degree that that begins to register with you, your life loses the sense of battle; it loses the struggle; and your good begins to appear by Grace, without taking thought for your life, "not by might, nor by power, but by my spirit,"[8] by the spirit of God that dwells in you. All this can happen only in proportion as you begin to know that you live as the Christ and to recognize your true identity, your Christhood.

I, my true identity, is the Christ.
The mind of the Christ is my mind;
the soul of God is my soul. I and the Father are one,
and all the spiritual qualities of the Father are mine.

Putting On the Robe

As you live with the recognition of your Christhood and as you meditate, then, in that inner stillness and peace, the "click" comes, that which happened to Moses when he could say, "I Am that I Am."[9] *I Am.* Jesus had that same realization, a realization which was the foundation of his whole ministry: "He that seeth me seeth him that sent me."[10] In that recognition he did not have to heal those who came clamoring to him because he knew that they also were this same Christ, and he knew that there are no evil powers, no negative powers. So his mighty works were done, and he lived his life by Grace as Jesus, the Christ.

When you take the name of the Christ, then live as that Christ-consciousness. Do not make a liar of yourself day in and day out; do not make that claim, and then turn around and act contrary to it. Once you claim the name of the Christ, live out from the Christ. "Wherefore if thy hand or thy foot offend thee, cut them off and cast them from thee. . . . And if thine eye offend thee, pluck it out, and cast it from thee,"[11] rather than surrender yourself and go back to being "man, whose breath is in his nostrils,"[12] rather than go back to being the carnal man.

Once you have recognized Christ as your identity, it is the equivalent of putting on the Robe. The Robe is not a material thing: the Robe is the spirit of Christ; the Robe is the consciousness of the Christ. When you have put that on, live up to it. You will not live up to it one hundred percent. No one can do that, but do not use that as an excuse to grovel in the dirt. Be up there to the very highest of your capacity, and stay there in your divine sonship. The son of God is raised up in you only when you acknowledge that you are He, that the son of God is your true identity.

Once you realize this Christ-identity, live with It internally, and anyone who wants to observe Its effects outwardly may do so. If your friends or acquaintances want to acknowledge, "Oh, you have something," or, "Oh, you are different," that is all right. But do not you claim the Christ, and do not tell them that they are It either, because this cannot be told to anyone except in proportion as a person has been raised up to receive It. There is enough animal nature in a human being so that he would enjoy telling you that you are wrong. The Master warns you of that: "Give not that which is holy unto the dogs, neither cast your pearls before swine."[13] Do not cast your spiritual wisdom before the unillumined thought. It will turn and rend you.

With the Recognition of Christhood, the Natural Man Dies

The more you recognize Christ as the identity of every individual, however, the less capacity he has left for being animalistic. That is what in this age is changing a great part of the world. Many who want to remain in their animal nature are having the capacity to be animalistic taken away from them by those who are seeing spiritually the true nature of man.

> I, myself, am the Christ-Self. I, myself, am the real man, the spiritual man, the Son of God. All that the Father has is mine: all the divine qualities, all the divine nature, all the divine being. This is the truth about me and the truth about every man.

The natural man comes along and says, "Ah, but"; and then that is when you, in your higher recognition, must turn and say, "'Get thee behind me, Satan!' I know all about the claims of Satan. I know all about the claims of the carnal man, but I stand on the dignity of my true nature. I know who I am."

In the proportion that you see that, you are meditating. This is contemplative meditation, and it leads to an inner stillness and quiet, and then sometime when you are not thinking at all, when you are not even thinking of meditating, all of a sudden the truth will pop up: "Knowest thou not, thou art the Christ of God? Knowest thou not, thou art the temple of God?"

You look up, "Who spoke; who spoke?" It was the "still small voice."[14] You brought yourself to an inner stillness where you could hear that Voice by this continued realization of your true identity.

Praying Without Ceasing by Abiding in Your Spiritual Identity

"A thousand shall fall at [the] side, and ten thousand at [the] right hand"[15] of those who dwell in the truth of spiritual identity. But if you live consciously in the realization of the Christ and let the Christ dwell in you as your Self, you will bear rich spiritual fruitage, because all that the Father has is yours as the Christ. Divine sonship is your relationship to God. The more you abide in this truth and let this truth abide in you, the more it will be so unto you. The less you let it occupy your consciousness, the less spiritual Grace you will know.

Whether you say, "Christ in the midst of me is mighty," whether you say, "I in the midst of me is mighty," whether you say, "Christ goes before me to make the 'crooked places straight,'"[16] or whether you say, "I go before me to make the 'crooked places straight,'" makes no difference because it is only a matter of terminology. You are recognizing your divine sonship, and this is what is necessary. You must know this truth without ceasing. You cannot wait for a problem to arise; you cannot wait for eight o'clock in the morning or seven o'clock at night. You can start that way as a young student, but you cannot remain that way for long. It must be a praying without ceasing; it must be a knowing of the truth; it must be an abiding in Bible passages and promises.

There must be a conscious dwelling in the realization of your true identity and the recognition that there is also a natural man hovering about. It will tempt you to be sick; it will tempt you to sin; it will tempt you to lose your temper, it will tempt you to do a lot of things; and some of them you will even fall for; but be assured that that natural man will have less and less place in your life as you abide more and more in the nature of your true identity. Know who you are, and live with it silently and secretly. Then you will know that *I* will never leave you or forsake you, because *I* am your Self. You can never be divided from your Self; and your Self is spiritual, divine sonship. To know this is illumination.

Which Is Your Way of Life?

There are two ways of life open to a person here on earth: there is the human way, the way of the unillumined, and there is the spiritual way, the way of the illumined. The difference between the individual who is living the ordinary human life and the one who is living the spiritual life is not quite as mysterious as it may seem to be. Living the spiritual life does not remove one, necessarily, from normal home or professional activities. It is merely the introduction into daily living of a new note, a different note.

Most persons are born into this world in the unillumined state, and there they remain throughout this entire period of human experience. The choice between living in the unillumined or in the illumined state does not rest with a human being, however, and if he turns to the spiritual path it is clearly not of his own volition: it is a divine Grace that touches him and moves him in this direction. Everyone would be on the spiritual path if he could be. The spiritual path is a way of joy, peace, and dominion over the things of life; it is a way of harmony, of rest, and very often of prosperity. Are not these the things that everyone is seeking? The only difference is that there is the unillumined way of seeking them, and there is the illumined way. Fortunate are those who are touched sufficiently by Grace to enable them to seek the illumined way.

Just what is the difference between the unillumined and the illumined? The unillumined, the human being in his ordinary state, is an individual living his own life with no help from the divine Source, with no help outside his own wisdom, his own strength, his own choice, his own power. It is a difficult life, this life to which Adam was condemned because he came to know good and evil: "In the sweat of thy face shalt thou eat bread."[17] It is a life of toil, effort, and worry. An individual living a human life has no recourse to anyone or to anything but his own powers. He may be limited in education, limited in experience, limited in background, or limited in finances. All kinds of limitation may restrict the life of the unillumined and prevent his attaining the peace, health, prosperity, and dominion promised the heirs of God.

The New Dimension of the Illumined

The illumined are illumined only for one reason: a new dimension has entered their experience. This new dimension has already been referred to in the August letter as the realization of God or the activity of the Christ. What it really means is that the individual, who one day was living his own life, alone, within himself, relying on his own powers, all of a sudden becomes aware of a Presence, a Power, a Something. Most of the time it cannot be defined, more especially when it first happens, but it is an instinct, an intuition, a feeling, an awareness that there is Something more to his life than what meets the eye, more than the personal sense of self. Something is with him; Something is protecting him; Something is giving him enlightenment, wisdom, guidance, and direction, even in the mundane affairs of life. Christ Jesus called this Something the Father within: "The Father that dwelleth in me, he doeth the works."[18]

Saul of Tarsus, in that moment on the road to Damascus when he was stricken blind, became aware of the Presence. From then on, he was being instructed from within and was being given light from within. He went away for many years to ponder the experience, to let it come to maturity, and when he started out on his ministry, he was able to say that what he did, he did through the Christ. "I can do all things through Christ which strengtheneth me.[19] . . . I live; yet not I, but Christ liveth in me."[20] Under his new name of Paul, he realized: "I am not alone. The whole of what I was seeking was contact with that which I now realize is within me and with which I tabernacle, with which I can commune, to which I can go for refuge, safety, security, guidance, wisdom, and instruction."

So the life of Christ Jesus and the life of Paul both testify to the fact that from the moment of their conscious awareness of an overbrooding Presence within, life changes, values change, and all that heretofore has been sought in the without is now sought and found within.

I, too, can say that it is the Father within that has given me this message to teach, that has given me this spiritual discernment with which to bear witness to the healing and regenerative power of the Spirit. "The Spirit of the Lord is upon me, because he hath anointed me,"[21] and I am ordained to heal the sick. Do you notice that always there is this recognition of this Something, this Otherness, this Withinness.

The Divine Companion Fulfills Every Need

The Master has been described as a lonely man. Paul's entire life was also lonely, with no one really to understand him or his mission, and yet there was no sorrow in this, because there was always this inner communion, this inner tabernacling with the divine Companion. Every relationship of life can be found in the companionship of this inner Presence, even as Isaiah said, "Thy Maker is thine husband."[22]

The mystics of the Old Testament described this divine Companion as a fortress, a high tower, a hiding place, an abiding place. "He that dwelleth in the secret place of the most High shall abide under the shadow of the Almighty. . . . There shall no evil befall thee, neither shall any plague come nigh thy dwelling."[23] But the dwelling place of the person who expects to enjoy this security must be the kingdom of God within, not living any more in the external, yet not leaving it.

To be in the world but not of it means to live your daily life as you are accustomed to living it, but without concern and without believing that the values of life are external to you. You are not to believe that your safety or security is in anything in the external world. If you need a fortress, God will be your fortress. If you need a hiding place, God will be your hiding place.

The Master reveals, "I am the bread of life."[24] If you need bread, God will be the bread. Do you need to be resurrected out of your sins, your diseases, your lacks? Then God must be the resurrection. When you find yourself in God or when you find your home in Him, when you realize that divine Presence that is within you and learn to commune and tabernacle with It, to pray in, through, and with It, everything in the outer world conforms to this inner pattern. All things work together for good in the outer picture; the whole outer picture conforms to one of harmony and peace.

What a difference between that man who lives in God and that self, alone and unaware of this spiritual Presence filling all space within and without! What worries, concerns, and fears there are when life is lived separate and apart from the Presence! Those fears are the fears of "the natural man [who] receiveth not the things of the Spirit of God,"[25] the natural man who is not "subject to the law of God, neither indeed can be."[26] His worries, doubts, and fears are natural, but how quickly these evaporate and disappear in the life experience of the same individual in that moment when it is revealed to him: "*I* am in the midst of you. *I* will never leave you, nor forsake you. *I* will be with you unto the end of the world. Rest in *Me,* rest in this Word."

The weight falls from the shoulders; the lines leave the forehead. There is no longer fear. How can you fear what mortal man can do when there is a divine Grace within you? How can you fear the external world, the world of effect, when you have within yourself this Presence which is omnipotence, all-power, divine power, spiritual power? Can you fear any form of temporal power in the presence of divine power?

There Is No Mystery About Illumination to the Illumined

Gain a fuller understanding of what temporal power means and then realize the nature of spiritual power that operates, "not by might, nor by power, but by my spirit," the Spirit which is within you, with which you have been ordained. It is this consciousness of the presence and the power of God within that constitutes illumination.

To many the language of the spiritual world is strange and mysterious, but that is only because they do not yet know its meaning. In my younger years, I used to stand sometimes behind the scenes of a vaudeville house when Harry Houdini was performing, and to me he was the greatest miracle worker of all time, greater than anybody who ever lived or would live. But not so to himself: there was nothing mysterious or great about what he was doing. He was applying certain principles which he understood. Only to those who were in darkness insofar as magic was concerned, were his tricks difficult and mysterious.

So also to the illumined there is no mystery about the word, "illumination," or about the term, "the Christ," or "the spirit of God that dwelleth in me." It is simple. It means only that there is a Something. No one has ever been able to define It, analyze It, or name It. It is Spirit. It is incorporeal. No one has ever seen It, heard It, tasted It, touched It, smelled It, or even been able to think about It. It is just Something that is, and you are aware that It is; you are aware that It is within you, that It walks beside you, that It is a rear guard to protect you, and goes ahead to make the crooked places straight, to prepare mansions for you.

The Fruitage of Spiritual Awareness

You may at first intellectually agree that the great mystics spoke truly when they spoke of a Presence within. You may intellectually agree that God has provided you from the beginning with His Son, His Son in the midst of you, but this acknowledgment can be only a first step on the path. From now on, you tabernacle with this revelation; you commune within yourself; you think; you ponder; you meditate upon this idea until in a sudden moment it dawns.

> It is true! The spirit of the Lord God is upon me;
> His spirit is within me; His Grace is my sufficiency
> in all things; and this Grace is here where I am.

If this revelation of divine sonship finds a man in prison, it will soon release him. If this finds a person in sin, it will quickly purify him. If this finds a person in disease, it will heal him. If it finds him in lack, in limitation, or in unhappiness, it will free him, for "where the Spirit of the Lord is, there is liberty,"[27] When this Spirit finds an individual in bondage—political, physical, mental, moral, financial, it makes no difference what the bondage—It operates at once to set him free.

The mission of this spirit of God in man is to bring forth freedom. "I am come," this spirit of God declares unto you, "I am come in the midst of you that you might have life, and that you might have the life abundant." Where the spirit of the Lord is, there is your freedom from bondage of any name or nature. There is your freedom from lack, limitation, and fear. Above all, the realization of this indwelling Presence is your freedom from temporal power. No weapon, then, that is formed against you can prosper. No weapon!

Weapons that are formed against you as a human being do prosper, but from the moment of the realization of this spirit of the Lord God that is upon you, no weapon that is formed against you can prosper, because that weapon is not formed against you, but against the Christ. It does not reach you: it reaches that Christ or spirit of God and is instantly dissolved. No weapon that is formed against the Christ can prosper. "Thou couldest have no power at all against me, except it were given thee from above."[28] If the Master had not consented to his own crucifixion for some purpose of his own, Pilate could never have completed the task. The reason this is true is that no weapon that is formed against the spiritual presence of God can prosper, for God is omnipotence, all-power.

Since the spirit of God includes freedom, it is comforting to remember that no weapon that is formed against man's freedom can prosper. This immediately dissolves his fears of temporal powers, domestic and foreign, and always the miracle of freedom will take place through some normal, natural way in the human picture.

The unillumined individual is a person living by and through his own powers, wisdom, and strength. The illumined is living in conscious awareness of an indwelling Presence, Being, Power. The individual has received illumination in that moment when he realizes:

> I am not living my life alone.
> I live, yet not I; this spirit of the Lord God
> which is upon me is living my life.

Gross materialism has reversed the secret of supply. Supply is not getting, not even in the human realm. Supply is giving, sharing, bestowing. It is only in the measure of your outpouring that you have an infinite amount of supply. I grant that only spiritual light and spiritual illumination reveal this, because materialistic sense has reversed it, and in doing so, has made many persons poor. This belief that getting makes rich and brings supply has caused much poverty on earth. So many who have succeeded in gaining wealth have found that when they have it, it was dust because it was not supply. It did not bring them what supply is supposed to bring: infinite good.

What do you want of supply? What do you want of money if it is not an abundance of life, and life with health, peace, and happiness? You have learned that money does not buy these; therefore, money is not supply. Money is one of those effects of supply that comes to individuals in abundance when they have learned the spiritual law of supply, which is giving, sharing, bestowing.

The freedom you give to anyone is the freedom you attain. The freedom, the release, that you give to others is the freedom and release that returns to you. Through spiritual illumination you see that what you give returns to you. The education that you give another returns to you; the help you give another returns to you; the freedom you give others, setting them free from bondage to you in any form, is the freedom that returns to you. Since you are spiritual, you are that very center through which all of God's grace flows out to this universe.

When you think in terms of getting or receiving, you dam up the very avenues of supply that have been given you from the beginning of time. These avenues of supply are the outpouring of love and life, the outpouring of the Spirit, the outpouring of all good, freedom, joy, and bliss.

What you give is what you have; what you hold is what you lose. Why? Because in giving, the spirit of the Lord God is upon you, and it is this Spirit that is flowing out from you. Therefore, all this good that you give—the sharing, the releasing, the freeing—is not really of yourself: it is only that you have allowed yourself to be a transparency through which the grace of God may flow to this universe.

Spiritual illumination reveals that men and women as such are not good or evil, but rather that they are the instruments, channels, or transparencies through which love, truth, justice, mercy, and benevolence are to flow. They are never the instruments for evil, for evil is an impersonal nonentity; it is not of God, and that ends it. Only those who continue to accept this belief of personal good and personal evil continue either to benefit from it or suffer from it. In the moment that you realize, "Do not call me good. Please recognize that the spirit of God is flowing through me," you lift your eyes above your head, and say, "Thank You, Father, for unfolding and revealing truth."

So, too, you look above the heads of government with a "Thank You, Father, for justice, liberty, freedom, harmony, divine government," and looking up, realizing that these qualities and activities must flow forth from divine Consciousness through men, you will find that no man has the ability or capacity to withhold these things.

The day is fast going by, in fact, the day is past, when an individual controls the fate of other individuals; and that is because now there are enough persons on earth realizing that they need not fear what mortal man can do; they need not fear what mortal man can give or withhold, for there is a divine

Grace flowing directly from an infinite Consciousness through the transparency of mankind.

Never again fear "man, whose breath is in his nostrils." Do not fear the power of princes. There is a divine Consciousness closer to you than breathing. It is the source of infinite abundance; It has placed the crops in the ground, and the gold and the silver, the pearls in the sea, and all the treasures that have not yet been drawn forth from the air, the earth, and the sea. This infinite divine Consciousness is the source and the activity of your good. You see man now only as the instrument or transparency through which this divine Grace flows to you.

That which is not ordained of God cannot survive. No weapon that is formed against the Christ, against the qualities of justice, freedom, and equality can prosper, for God is infinite. God is omnipotence, omnipresence, omniscience. Besides God there is nothing; and God is in the midst of you. God is here and now.

It is illumination to awaken and realize that you are free; the fetters are fallen, man no longer binds you mentally or physically; man no longer restricts you; man no longer dominates you, because you are looking above the head of man or you are looking right through his eyes to the center of his soul or you are looking deep into his heart, and there you find this inner Presence. You rest in that Presence, and you cease concern about man. This is spiritual illumination. This is the difference between the unillumined who walk in doubt and fear, and the illumined who walk without fear, by Grace.

ACROSS THE DESK

As illumination brings a deeper awareness of the indwelling Christ, our hearts overflow with gratitude for God's great gift of grace. May the joy of that realization be yours this Christmas Day and may each day throughout the year be filled with Its peace.

About the Series

The 1971 through 1981 *Letters* will be published as a series of eleven fine-quality soft cover books. Each book published in the first edition will be offered by Acropolis Books and The Valor Foundation, and can be ordered from either source:

ACROPOLIS BOOKS, INC.
8601 Dunwoody Place
Suite 303
Atlanta, GA 30350-2509
(800) 773-9923
acropolisbooks@mindspring.com

THE VALOR FOUNDATION
1101 Hillcrest Drive
Hollywood, FL 33021
(954) 989-3000
info@valorfoundation.com

Scriptural References and Notes

CHAPTER ONE

1 John 18:36.
2 John 14:27.
3 Luke 12:22, 31.
4 Robert Browning.
5 John 8:11.
6 I John 3:2.
7 I Corinthians 3:16.
8 Exodus 3:5.
9 Luke 15:31.
10 John 10:30.
11 John 12:45.
12 Proverbs 3:6.
13 John 8:32.
14 Isaiah 45:2.
15 I Kings 19:12.

CHAPTER TWO

1 John 9:25.
2 From an inscription in the chapel at Stanford University, Palo Alto, California, quoted in the author's *The World Is New.* (New York, N.Y.: Harper and Row, 1962), P.7
3 I Corinthians 2:14.
4 Romans 8:7.
5 I Kings 19:11.
6 John 18:38.
7 John 14:6.
8 John 15:5,6.
9 Psalm 91:10.
10 Galatians 2:20.
11 Matthew 7:14.
12 John 18:36.
13 Matthew 26:52.
14 Isaiah 2:22.
15 I Samuel 3:9.
16 Isaiah 26:3.
17 Matthew 12:39.

[18] I Corinthians 3:16.
[19] I Corinthians 6:19.
[20] Romans 8:16.

CHAPTER THREE

[1] John 18:36.
[2] Matthew 4:4.
[3] Matthew 5:39.
[4] Matthew 26:52.
[5] Matthew 4:4.
[6] 1 Kings 19:12.
[7] Luke 17:21.
[8] John 4:24.
[9] Revelation 2:17.
[10] John 4:32.
[11] II Corinthians 12:7.
[12] Psalm 46:10.

CHAPTER FOUR

[1] Luke 23:24.
[2] Galatians 6:7,8.
[3] Ezekiel 18:32.
[4] Joshua 24:15.
[5] Matthew 28:7.
[6] John 8:32.

CHAPTER FIVE

[1] Ephesians 4:22.
[2] Philippians 2:5.
[3] Matthew 25:40.
[4] Galatians 6:7.
[5] Galatians 6:8.
[6] John 4:32.
[7] Revelation 2:17.
[8] Matthew 18:20.
[9] Romans 8:7.
[10] Isaiah 2:22
[11] Matthew 11:28.
[12] I Corinthians 2:14.
[13] Romans 8:20.
[14] John 10:10.
[15] Philippians 3:14.

CHAPTER SIX

[1] Isaiah 26:3.
[2] Proverbs 3:5,6.
[3] Job 23:14.
[4] Psalm 138:8.
[5] I John 4:4.
[6] John 10:30.
[7] John 5:30.
[8] John 14:10.
[9] Isaiah 45:2.
[10] Hebrews 13:5.
[11] John 18:36.
[12] John 1:17.
[13] Matthew 5:22.

14 Matthew 5:28.
15 Matthew 5:22.
16 Matthew 19:17.

CHAPTER SEVEN

1 Romans 12:2.
2 Acts 10:12.
3 Acts 10:14.
4 Acts 10:44.
5 Matthew 13:3-8.
6 Matthew 12:13.
7 John 11:41,42
8 John 11:43.
9 John 8:32.
10 Genesis 18:32.
11 John 15:16.

CHAPTER EIGHT

1 John 12:32.
2 John 10:30.
3 Mark 13:31.
4 Luke 23:34.
5 Galatians 2:20.
6 Isaiah 61:1.
7 Romans 8:11.
8 Matthew 5:39.
9 John 14:27
10 John 18:36.
11 Matthew 19:19.
12 Mark 16:17.

CHAPTER NINE

1 John 1:17.
2 Mark 2:27.
3 Hebrews 10:6.
4 I Corinthians 7:19.
5 Matthew 3:15.
6 John 4:21.
7 Luke 17:21.
8 Galatians 6:7.
9 Galatians 6:8.
10 Hebrews 13:5.
11 Psalm 23:4.
12 Matthew 22:37,39.
13 Psalm 147:5.
14 Psalm 24:1.
15 Luke 15:31.
16 Matthew 19:17.
17 John 5:30.
18 Galatians 2:20.

CHAPTER TEN

1 John 14:12.
2 Romans 7:19,20.
3 Exodus 3:14.
4 Matthew 25:40.
5 Acts 10:34.
6 Exodus 3:5.
7 Ephesians 6:12.
8 I Corinthians 15:31.
9 Luke 4:18.
10 Isaiah 2:22.

[11] Romans 6:16.
[12] Matthew 5:40.
[13] Psalm 24:1.
[14] Matthew 23:9.
[15] John 8:32.
[16] John 3:7.
[17] Acts 1:24.

CHAPTER ELEVEN

[1] Matthew 4:1-11.
[2] Luke 4:18,21.
[3] Matthew 13:46.
[4] John 16:33.
[5] John 10:30.

CHAPTER TWELVE

[1] John 15:15.
[2] I Corinthians 2:14.
[3] Luke 4:8.
[4] Matthew 26:40.
[5] Colossians 3:9,10.
[6] II Corinthians 5:4.
[7] Matthew 16:15.
[8] Zechariah 4:6.
[9] Exodus 3:14.
[10] John 12:45.
[11] Matthew 18:8,9.
[12] Isaiah 2:22.
[13] Matthew 7:6.
[14] I Kings 19:12.
[15] Psalm 91:7.
[16] Isaiah 45:2.
[17] Genesis 3:19.
[18] John 14:10.
[19] Philippians 4:13.
[20] Galatians 2:20.
[21] Luke 4:18.
[22] Isaiah 54:5.
[23] Psalm 91:1,10.
[24] John 6:35.
[25] I Corinthians 2:14.
[26] Romans 8:7.
[27] II Corinthians 3:17.
[28] John 19.11.

Joel Goldsmith
Tape Recorded Classes
Corresponding to the
Chapters of this Volume

~

Tape recordings may be ordered from

THE INFINITE WAY
PO Box 2089, Peoria AZ 85380-2089
Telephone 800-922-3195 Fax 623-412-8766

E-mail: infiniteway@earthlink.net
www.joelgoldsmith.com
Free Catalog Upon Request

CHAPTER 1: THE NOW ACTIVITY OF THE CHRIST
#456   1962 Glendale Open Class   1:1

CHAPTER 2: FIRST STEPS ON THE PATH OF DISCIPLESHIP
#491   1962 Manchester Closed Class   1:1

CHAPTER 3: THE SWORD OF THE SPIRIT
#527   1963 London Work   3:1

CHAPTER 4: LIFE UNFOLDING AS THE
            FRUITAGE OF ATTAINED CONSCIOUSNESS
#457   1962 Glendale Open Class   2:2

CHAPTER 5: PUTTING OFF THE OLD MAN AND REBIRTH

    #490   1962 London Closed Class   4:1

    #491   1962 Manchester Closed Class   1:2

CHAPTER 6: BUILDING THE TRANSCENDENTAL CONSCIOUSNESS

    #413   1961 Manchester Special Class   2:2

CHAPTER 7: PREPARATION FOR SPIRITUAL BAPTISM

    #416   1961 London Open Class   3:1

CHAPTER 8: THE FOURTH DIMENSION

    #230   1958 London Open Class   4:2

    #267   1959 Hawaiian Village

              Closed Class   6:2

CHAPTER 9: FROM HUMANHOOD TO DIVINITY

    #230   1958 London Open Class   4:2

    #445   1962 Hawaiian Village

              Open Class   2:2

CHAPTER 10: CALL NO MAN YOUR FATHER UPON THE EARTH

    #475   1962 Princess Kaiulani

              Closed Class   2:2

    #477   1962 Princess Kaiulani

              Closed Class   4:2

CHAPTER 11: TEACHER AND STUDENT ON THE PATH

#226   1958 London Closed Class   3:2
#490   1962 London Closed Class   4:1
#325   1960 Chicago Closed Class   1:1
#453   1962 Mission Inn Closed Class   3:2
#526   1963 London Work   2:1
#267   1959 Hawaiian Village
            Closed Class   6:2

CHAPTER 12: SPIRITUAL ILLUMINATION

#483   1962 Princess Kaiulani
            Closed Class   4:2
#444   1962 Hawaiian Village
            Open Class   1:2